RAIN
OR
SHINE

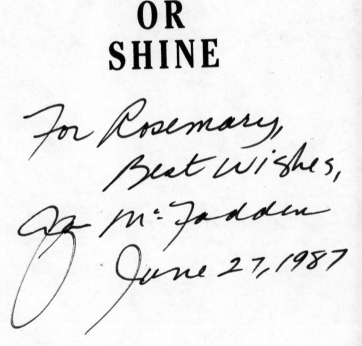

For Rosemary,
Best wishes,
Jay McFadden
June 27, 1987

Also by Cyra McFadden

THE SERIAL

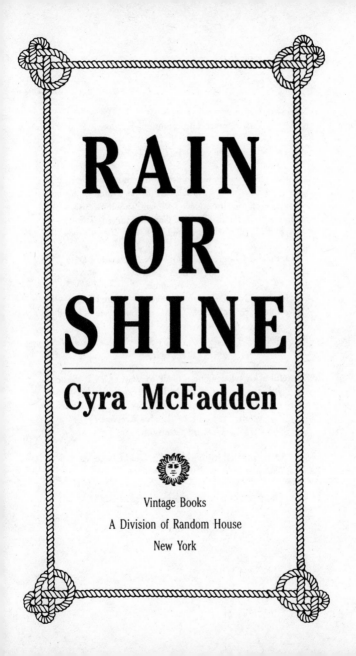

RAIN OR SHINE

Cyra McFadden

Vintage Books

A Division of Random House

New York

First Vintage Books Edition, July 1987

Library of Congress Cataloging-in-Publication Data
McFadden, Cyra.
Rain or shine.
1. Taillon, Cy. 2. Rodeo announcers—United States—
Biography. 3. McFadden, Cyra. 4. Journalists—United
States—Biography. I. Title.
GV742.42.T35M34 1987   070.4′497918 [B]   86-46171
ISBN 0-394-74879-4

Grateful acknowledgment is made to Warner Bros. Music
Inc. for permission to reprint an excerpt from
"Don't Fence Me In" by Cole Porter. Copyright 1944 (renewed)
Warner Bros. Inc. All rights reserved.
Used by permission.

DESIGNED BY JO ANNE METSCH

FOR KENT

ACKNOWLEDGMENTS

Without the help of my brothers Terry
and Tom Taillon, who gave me access
to our father's files and scrapbooks, I
could not have written this book. They
have my gratitude as well as my love.

RAIN
OR
SHINE

INTRODUCTION

When my father died, in April of 1980, newspapers in the West compared him with John Wayne. "Cy Taillon was more than a rodeo announcer," said the writer for the Miles City *Star* in Miles City, Montana, "like John Wayne was more than an actor. Each became an embodiment of an ideal, a spokesman for a quality of life and a way of living it." America was younger when my father left his family's North Dakota farm and Wayne left the football field of the University of Southern California, the writer continued. "It took men of iron will, stout hearts and sensitive manner to tame her. Stubborn men who spoke their minds and minded what they spoke. Times have changed, so has America. And so has rodeo."

He's right about America and rodeo. My father never changed, not in his loyalty to Western values. When his Denver house was burglarized of two hundred dollars' worth of appliances several years ago, he told the Denver *Post*, "I plan to have an armed resident in the house with orders to shoot first and argue later."

Cy was at the top of his profession then. In fact he was the top, with no competition for his title "Dean of Rodeo Announcers," an accolade accorded him by the rest of the rodeo world and almost always attached to his name. Once a rakehell, he'd been respected and respectable for thirty years: well paid, happily married, a family man and a householder. But inside him, beneath his custom-tailored Western jackets, beat the heart of a cowboy. No one stole his toaster while he was out on the road, if he could help it, and walked away intact. A shotgun shell or two should handle the problem nicely.

We were not speaking to each other then. His blue-eyed darling as a child, named after him, dressed like him as a wrong-sex, unusually short cowboy, I'd grown up, moved away from Montana, moved away in heart and mind from my father and shoot first, argue later. I had a couple of degrees, a divorce behind me and a second marriage; a suburban California house; belonged to the ACLU; took part in San Francisco peace marches while my half brother by my father's second marriage was fighting in Vietnam and my father editorializing from the crow's nest, the rodeo announcer's booth, in support of the war.

The last time we'd seen each other, he and I argued about racial intermarriage, hippies, Catholicism as the one true religion and what to have for dinner. We were at an elegant San Francisco

Chinese restaurant. My father insisted that we both eat chow mein. I was full of self and my new sophistication and didn't want to sit at the same table with a man who'd order chow mein at Kan's. Especially a man in kangaroo-skin cowboy boots, nipped-in Western suit and diamond pinkie ring.

We were obnoxious in equal proportions, but my father won. He had a voice that could fill a football stadium without amplification, and he was picking up the check.

So he went back to embodying the West while I went back to ACLU meetings. We exchanged letters in which we discussed politics and each other's character defects. Then we exchanged no letters at all, keeping track of each other through relatives, waiting for the other to heal the rift. Cy Taillon's daughter, I am as stubborn as he was. We loved each other, missed each other, and made ourselves miserable, and this went on for years, time for our grievances to harden into granite.

I rankled at a distance about the form my father's letters took, when I was still receiving them. He sent me a carbon of the letters he wrote his entire family. It was a large family. He always sent me the blurry last carbon.

His own grievances predated our quarrel about San Francisco and whether or not it was part Sodom, part Gomorrah. As a child, I used to meet my father on the rodeo circuit in the summers, in Billings or Miles City or Lewiston, traveling by Greyhound bus, a label pinned to my shirt: "If bus isn't met deliver to Cy Taillon, fairgrounds." On each such occasion, he marched me off instantly to a beauty shop to have a permanent wave, frustrated beyond tolerance that no matter who did what to me, and no matter how much he paid for it, my hair refused to curl. He wanted a daughter who looked like Shirley Temple. Instead, he had a sulky, waiflike child who looked more like Oliver Twist.

The afternoon before we met for dinner at Kan's, he'd made one more attempt. "Go get your hair done," he said, and gave me twenty dollars. At the beauty shop in his San Francisco hotel, a hairdresser tormented me into a lofty bouffant. I felt freakish, and it didn't help our relations that my father was once again disappointed. "I give up," he said when he saw me. I had to put on my dark glasses. Crying, I had been taught long ago, was for sissies.

We were a long time reconciling, and when reconciliation came, it came on my father's terms. He was sick and demoralized after a small stroke. A letter turned up in my mailbox, on his flamboyant stationery, with its cowboy hat, microphone and lariat logo and the legend: "Cy Taillon, Master of Ceremonies and Rodeo Announcer, with records unequaled for consecutive engagements." He wrote that he'd been hoping for a move from me for years, feeling that "any desire to communicate" should originate with me because he was blameless in our estrangement.

I raged at his tone of injured merit; thought about how he always told reporters he had two children, my two half brothers, Terry and Tommy, and not three; remembered every hurt, every slight, and how, when Cy finally left his tempestuous marriage to my mother, he quickly began the process of erasing me from the record of his life along with her.

When we were together, he sometimes slipped and called me "Pat." I was the living reminder that he'd once slept with her, caroused with her, been deeply and destructively in love with her. Respectability had come late and hard to him. I remembered the person he'd been—dazzling, reckless, a drunk.

The day his letter came, I phoned him, and the voice that had made him famous resonated over the line. Majestically, he told me that if I apologized, he was willing to forgive me. He was, he said, incapable of holding a grudge.

We had nine years to make our peace before cancer killed him. I wrote a book during that time, was interviewed by reporters myself and began to tell the ones who asked me where I got my odd name that my father invented it. He was Cy Taillon, Dean of the Rodeo Announcers and living Western legend.

That he was pleased, Terry and Tommy assure me. He also kept articles that I wrote and sent and newspaper pieces in which I mentioned him. What he wrote me was that he was pleased my book was doing well but that the attention paid to it surprised him. He was a writer, too, for Western periodicals, with files full of fan letters. He'd never received as much press as I did, for what was after all a short book. I must have a very good press agent.

In the summer two years after he died, I went back to Montana. This time I went to Great Falls, where my father died and my two brothers live. (I'm dropping "half brother" at this point because we're related not just by blood but by our complicated love for our father.) There I went on a pilgrimage of sorts with Terry, then thirty-seven and a rodeo announcer himself.

Cy was dead. My stepmother, Dorothy, was dead. My mother was failing and close to dying. Even more than Terry did, I felt cut loose from my life as I'd known it until then because my husband of twenty years had died the December before.

In Terry's new Buick Skylark, named "Ol' Sorrel Top," we headed for the Miles City Bucking Horse Sale, the last of Cy's unequaled consecutive engagements. Though Miles City has a celebrated rodeo, our real reason for the trip was to spend time together and to build a bridge between our vastly different lives.

Forty-four-year-old woman, widowed, an urban dweller; kid brother, now grown up and graying, big, barrel-chested, a cowboy. To make the trip and the bridge building go more smoothly, Terry set the car on cruise control and stopped only at crossroads bars.

The road from Great Falls to Miles City heads south across barren, empty country. We peeled away the miles with Jack Daniel's for me and Black

Velvet for Terry, while Willie Nelson sang old Hank Williams songs on the tape deck. After spending most of his life on the road, traveling with Cy and then making the circuit himself as a bronc rider, Terry is an expert in dead-animal identification, needing only a blot on the highway, a bit of entrail or a couple of tail feathers, to say authoritatively, "That's your coney" or "That's your magpie."

He said little else as we rolled along, other than "How do you like all this nothing?"

I said it was beautiful nothing. I'd missed it. I also said I wished my husband could have seen it.

"He's seeing it now," Terry said. Full of Jack Daniel's and strong feeling, I had to jam on my dark glasses again.

I did not believe that my dead husband, a man without a religious impulse, was hovering over the road to Miles City and listening, with Terry and me, to Willie Nelson. I also knew that Terry not only believes in heaven, he knows it looks just like Montana.

This book is a memoir of my father's life on the rodeo circuit, his marriage to my mother and my effort to understand the ways in which I am their daughter, who left the West and the world of rodeo behind, full of fear and loathing, to find that Cy Taillon's imprint was indelible. The first writing he ever published was satire; so was mine. We look alike, more so as I get older. Like my father, I love the road show, packing a bag, heading off somewhere or nowhere, traveling light, never looking back over my shoulder. All three of Cy's children, my brothers and I, have the rhythm of the road throbbing in our inner ears, seductive and disorienting if we have to stay in one place for long.

Recently, a friend pointed out to me something obvious I had not realized and found mildly clinical. The daughter of the man with a pipe organ in his throat, a voice that filled me with awe and thrilled audiences, I gravitate toward men with deep, resonant voices. The last time I spoke to him, I knew Cy was dying because his voice on the phone was thin, the cancer having attacked his vocal cords, and the voice was the man. Without it, there would have been no Cy Taillon, no outpouring of tributes when he died, no Dean of Rodeo—a sport that grew more respectable as my father did—championing it articulately, insisting that cowboys were professional athletes instead of hell-raising gypsies.

Our problem with each other was that I loved the hell-raising gypsy who had disappeared, as the years went by, behind reputation and money, the stability of his second marriage and his increasingly John Wayne–like views of how the world should work.

He thought men should be manly, in the traditional Western mold. Women should be their better halves, a role my mother found less than congenial. Male children should call their fathers "sir" and toe the line like West Point cadets. Daughters should defer to them, in matters of politics, religion and what to order from a Chinese menu. Their hair ought to curl.

I became respectable too, though I never deferred to Cy about much of anything, but like him, and like my mother, I prefer the night lights and the bright lights to the daylight, moving restlessly down the road to staying put. It's hereditary, I excuse myself, and fight the pull of the road, the cowboy bars and the signs I pass driving across California, going to visit a friend or carry out a writing assignment: "Oakhurst Rodeo, Saturday and Sunday."

That's going to be a good one, I think. Rowdy and dusty. No sixty-thousand-dollar-a-year all-American saddle-bronc riders. No NBC television cameras. Instead, heat and beer and animal smells, and cowboys from miles around convening in a small town to ride their hearts out and the seats of their pants off. I grip the wheel and keep going only because whoever is announcing, it won't be my father, and unless it's Terry, who says it can't be done, no one will ever preside over the crow's nest with the same style and presence.

Rodeo goes on, better attended and more popular all the time. My brothers' lives go on, and mine does, and through us, our father's name; it's still difficult to pay for a drink, in a Western bar, if your last name is or once was Taillon. But when the Miles City *Star* headlined its editorial: "The Voice of the Bucking Horse Sale Is Stilled," it marked not only the end of a man but the end of an era.

Rodeo won't have another senior statesman. Popular mythology aside, there aren't that many

gentleman cowboys, perhaps because the gentleman part rubs against the grain, and though some
of them are good at what they do, the announcers
who now travel my father's old routes aren't in his
one-man category. They lack his showmanship and
his patrician style.

In Sparks, Nevada, on my way home from Montana, I watched the movie *The Electric Horseman*
on television in my air-conditioned motel room,
still suspended between Miles City and San Francisco, my old life and the one I lead now. I'd seen
it before, but this time it stirred me, with its ele-
giac theme of a West once wild and now paved
over, once free-spirited and now tame.

Sunny, the broken-down cowboy hero, was rem-
iniscing about his days as a rodeo rider and about
Clark Wembley, an announcer with a "voice like
runnin' molasses." He made the cowboys, winners
and losers, feel special, Sunny says. He encouraged
them.

Clark Wembley was Cy Taillon, I knew, and I
remembered one of my father's surefire crowd
pleasers, a line that rumbled out from the booth
over big- and small-town arenas and was followed,
after a still moment, by thunderous noise. "Ladies
and gentlemen, this cowboy's only pay this afternoon is your applause."

Though the crowd had heard this staple of his
repertory a hundred times, and so had I, it always
brought us to our feet clapping until our hands
ached.

ONE

When they were young, my parents believed they were indestructible, so fast and flashy nothing could touch them. Cy was a lady-killer, a small, natty man whose riverboat-gambler good looks struck women down like lightning bolts. My mother, the former Patricia Montgomery, was a vaudeville dancer, the star of the St. Louis Municipal Opera in the late twenties. When she married Cy, she turned trick rider in the rodeo equivalent of half-time shows. You can take the girl out of show biz, but you cannot take a little girl from Little Rock, or Paragould, which is close enough, and turn her into a house pet.

At least not Pat, with her performer's ego, her longing to shine. Tiny-waisted and white-skinned, her black hair slicked to her cheekbones in sculptured spit curls, she was Cy's equal in recklessness, matching him drink for drink, seduction for seduction, irrational impulse for irrational impulse. Together they shot off sparks and left behind scorched earth, and if they ever thought about how their travels might end, they didn't waste much time on sober reappraisal.

They had more pressing concerns, the main one how to get to the next town with little money, a child and hangovers. My father's schedule took him from Butte, Montana, to Salt Lake City, Utah, from Puyallup, Washington, to Baton Rouge, Louisiana, and sometimes the travel time was a couple of days. We lived in a 1937 blue Packard, spending endless, viciously hot days in it going from Canada to New Mexico and back up to Wyoming, Utah and Idaho—wherever there were rodeos. We slept in that car, ate breakfast, lunch and dinner in it, sang along with the Sons of the Pioneers in it, quarreled in it. My parents must have made love in it, when I was asleep and the Packard parked behind the bleachers in some small-town fairground, waiting for daylight and the rodeo. Between them, there was a strong erotic pull. They walked with their hips touching and had flaming fights over each other's real and imagined flirtations.

Raised on a North Dakota farm, one of nine children of a French Canadian family, Cy had been a law student, a self-taught musician who led dance bands and played in movie-theater pit orchestras, a boxer and a radio personality in Billings and Salt Lake City. In both towns, he was a celebrity, known as "The Singing Announcer" because until a tonsillectomy put an end to this facet of his career, he sang with his bands.

The huge leather scrapbooks he kept all his life document some of these successes; but he claimed triumphs in everything he did, telling a writer for a trade paper called *Hoofs and Horns,* early in his rodeo career, that he'd won a Golden Gloves championship when he was boxing and given a recital at Carnegie Hall as a child prodigy violinist.

How much of that interview is true, I don't know, nor do I think Cy did. For much of his life, he was engaged in the game of inventing himself— adding to what was true what was desirable, stirring counterclockwise and serving up the mix. He must have swallowed much of it himself.

What is fact is that after leaving law school with a theatrical troupe, he ended up, in his early twenties, in Great Falls, where he became a radio announcer and moonlighted as a musician. His hillbilly band, reported the Great Falls *Tribune,* drew 14,600 letters to the local radio station in six and a half weeks. This was roughly half the population of Great Falls at the time. It must have been a letter-writing town.

After two months in St. Paul, Minnesota, as "announcer and entertainer," Cy came back to Great Falls, and in 1929 was leading a trio during the dinner hour at the Hotel Rainbow and picking up other band jobs around town. "The Green Mill gardens, dinner and dancing resort on the paved extension of Second Avenue North, will be formally opened tonight. Eddie Stamy will be director of the orchestra that will play for at least four dances a week. Cy Taillon, Minneapolis, who han-

dles the drums, violin, bells, piano, and most anything else, is charged with providing the sweet
numbers."

"Cy Taillon and his orchestra will entertain you
again at the Crystal Ballroom . . . Featuring 'The
Crystal Ballroom Red Jackets.' "

"Tree Claim Park presents Cy Taillon and his
'Rocky Mountaineers.' Master of Ceremonies,
Waddie Ginger, Admission 50 cents."

To the list of instruments he played, another ad
for a resort added xylophone, banjo and "relatively
smaller string instruments."

The woman who became Cy's second wife got
her first glimpse of him during those days. She was
a schoolgirl. He was playing one of the twin pianos
in the window of a music store. Their eyes met,
she told me, and it was Romeo and Juliet, only
more intense. If my mother got in their way for
twelve years, that was only because Dorothy was
fourteen at the time. My father also had his hands
full with other women.

A personal archivist, Cy kept copies of every
letter he ever wrote, including one to the city at-
torney of Great Falls in those years. A woman was
harassing him, he complained, accusing him of
being the third party in a "spiritual triangle" and
fathering her three children by remote control.
"Further proof she is hopelessly irrational," he
wrote, "is her obsession that I have money."

In my teens, I met a woman who knew Cy in
Great Falls. "He was the most beautiful man who

ever lived," she said. "You don't look very much like him."

She wasn't rude so much as disappointed. I offered to say hello to him for her.

"He wouldn't remember me. There were too many of us. I'll tell you what, though, say hello for the Willis sisters and let him wonder which one."

The student's pilot license Cy took out in 1933 lists his age as twenty-five, weight 139 pounds, height five feet seven and three-quarters inches, hair black and eyes gray-green. It doesn't describe the movie-star handsomeness of his regular features, his olive skin, his wavy black hair and those eyes—as slate green as the ocean, and when he was angry, as cold.

He looked enough like Robert Taylor to double for him, later, in the riding scenes of the movie *Billy the Kid.*

Rodeo stock producer Leo Cremer tapped him for the crow's nest in the early thirties. Cy left radio for what he said was a three months' leave and never went back. Cremer was famous for his Brahma bulls, whose average weight was three-quarters of a ton: Black Devil, Yellow Jacket, Deer Face, Tornado, Joe Louis, Dynamite. He also had good instincts when he signed my father, despite Cy's reputation as a hard drinker and man-about-town.

Because he'd been attracted to it since his childhood, "Roman riding" the horses on the family farm, Cy was a natural for rodeo. He'd mainly swallowed a lot of dust. After he broke a shoulder, he gave up any ambition to be another Casey Tibbs.

He had cards printed, giving his address as the Mint Cafe, Great Falls, and offering "a New Technique in Rodeo Announcing."

A rodeo announcer keeps up a running commentary on the cowboys and the way they fare in the events, calf roping, Brahma-bull riding, bareback and saddle-bronc riding and, more recently, team roping. Cy was the best, a showman who could play a crowd the way he played stringed instruments, by instinct and with perfect pitch. At the piano, he held to the theory that the more keys you used, the better you played. At the mike, he also used the equivalent of all the pedals. "Ladies and gentlemen, this next waddie broke his wrist and three ribs down in Abilene a few weeks ago, and now he's back in competition. That's called courage in my book. Tiny Rios out of Tulsa, Oklahoma, on a mean hunk of horseflesh called Son of Satan . . . Let's give him a little encouragement."

From his law school days, when he won prizes in debate, he had a sophisticated vocabulary. He used it, never talking down to his audience of cowboys, stock producers and their wives, ranchers and rodeo-loving kids. Nor did he often forget a cowboy's name, or where he came from, or how he fared in previous rodeos, no matter how chronic a loser the cowboy. So they loved him, even when he borrowed their prize money or their wives. He always paid the money back, and the wives straggled home, moony but unrepentant, on their own.

The reviews began to come in early. Cy never got a bad one, any more than he ever took an unflattering photograph, or if there were any, they never wound up in his scrapbooks, a researcher's nightmare because he clipped articles without the name of the newspaper or magazine and frequently without the date. Sometimes he clipped only the paragraphs that mentioned his name, which he underlined. The articles describe him as silver-voiced, golden-voiced, gold-and-silver-voiced, crystal-voiced, honey-voiced. They talk about his clear, bell-like voice. They run out of adjectives and call him the Voice.

In them, he's also spare, handsome and hard as nails; lean, wiry and a natty dresser; suave and dapper; the man who knows rodeo; the possessor of an encyclopedic memory. Said one writer, consigned to anonymity by my father's clipping methods, "Taillon keeps the show going like a golf ball swatted down a concrete highway."

Rodeo was used to announcers who treated the sport as a Wild West show, part vaudeville, part circus. Cy dignified it, with his ten-dollar words, his impeccably tailored, expensive suits and his insistence that the cowboys were professional athletes. When he intoned, "Ladies and gentlemen," women became ladies and men became gentlemen; the silver-tongued devil in the announcer's box, as often as not a rickety structure over the chutes and open to the rain, spoke with unmistakable authority. In a world where pretending to be an insider earns the outsider dismissal faintly underlined with menace, he counted as a working cowboy, though he earned his living with his mouth rather than his muscle.

Like the contestants, he lived from rodeo to rodeo, making just enough money to keep us in gas and hamburgers. He worked in all weather: heat, cold, freak rainstorms that turned arenas into mudholes. If he had extra money, everybody drank, and when we rented a room in a motor court, a luxury, cowboys bunked on the floor with their saddles for pillows. Despite his slight frame, he never hesitated about piling in when there was a fight; you had to get through him to get to somebody bigger, and because he was light on his feet and fast with his fists, few made it. Someone wading into my father also had to take on my mother, not one to sit on the sidelines letting out ladylike cries of dismay. A hundred-pound woman can do substantial damage with teeth, fingernails and a high-heeled shoe, and Pat had an advantage going in. No man would hit her back, though she was swearing ripely and trying to maim him, because no self-respecting Western man hits a lady.

The bars were my parents' living rooms. We spent our nights in them, our mornings in the Packard or a motor court—with Cy and Pat sleeping off their headaches and begging me to stop that goddamn humming—and our afternoons at the

Black Hills Roundup or the Snake River Stampede, rodeos that blur into one.

Pat sat in the bleachers, if she wasn't trick riding. I sat in the crow's nest with Cy, sometimes announcing the Grand Entry or the national anthem for him or testing the p.a. system. "One two three four, testing testing testing." I wanted to be a movie star. Cy said you had to start somewhere.

The high point of those afternoons, for me, was when Cy played straight man for the rodeo clowns, who sometimes railed at him because he wouldn't allow off-color material, the crude jokes that were a staple. Not present just to entertain, the clowns also divert the bulls or horses when a rider is down. The cowboys and the crowd love and respect them. So did I, and when my father bantered with them from the stand, he took on added luster.

Pinky Gist and his two mules, Mickey and Freckles, George Mills, John Lindsay, the great Emmett Kelly and a dozen others—sad-faced men in baggy pants, absurdly long shoes and long underwear, out in the arena, and my father aiding and abetting them:

"Eddie, there are ladies present here today. Would you mind pulling up your pants?"

"Sure, Cy." Eddie did a flawless double take, pulled his pants up and doffed his porkpie hat to my father. When he lifted the hat, his pants fell down again, revealing long johns with a trapdoor.

"I'm sorry, Cy. I was asleep in the barrel over there and a train hit me. It tore the buttons off my suspenders."

"That wasn't a train, Eddie," Cy said, kingly at the microphone. "That was a two-thousand-pound Brahma bull, and there's another one coming out of the chute right now."

Eddie screamed hoarsely, stumbled across the arena, clutched at his pants and fell over his shoes. "I wondered why I never heard the whistle."

No matter how many times I heard these routines, they never paled for me. Such is the power of early-childhood conditioning that I still love slapstick; mine is the lone voice laughing at a club act in which the comic gets hit with a pie.

I'm less taken with exhibition roping. The great trick-rope artist on the circuit was Monty Montana, a handsome man who could do anything with a rope, including roping Cy Taillon's daughter. On my father's command, I pretended to be a calf; bolted through a string barrier and into the arena; ran like mad until Monty lassoed me, ran down his rope, threw me and tied me. He never hurt me. The crowd loved it. I hated it.

Not to be upstaged, Pat sometimes followed with her breakneck trick riding—headstands at the gallop, vaulting to the ground from a standing position in the saddle. She was so fearless that the cowboys gathered at the fence to watch her, wondering if this would be the night Cy's crazy wife killed herself.

I still have part of her trick-riding costume, a red Spanish bolero with white scrollwork, silver spurs with tooled-leather straps and canted-heel boots. The full-sleeved white satin shirt disappeared, as did the high-waisted red pants that would fit a twelve-year-old boy. Pat's life in those years is recorded in a few bits of her rodeo wardrobe, her own mutilated scrapbook, in which she also obliterated the supporting cast, and not much else.

Constants from those countless rodeos: the smell of sweat and horses that rose out of the open stalls, just below the booth; the fine dust that floated over the arena, powdering evenly cowboys, animals, the crowd, my father's suit and his pointy-toed boots; the haze of cigarette smoke over the stands; the whinnying of horses, the bawling of calves and howling of dogs, left in pickup trucks out in the parking lot.

Always present too were the high voices of women, wives and girlfriends and rodeo groupies, the "buckle bunnies" who were, and are still, the wives' natural enemies. They set the standards of female dress, with their starched curls and their pinkish pancake makeup, ending in a line at the chin. The buckle bunnies wore tight frontier pants and tooled-leather belts, into which they tucked their nailhead-studded shirts. One who was always around, and whom I admired, had a belt with beads spelling out her name, just above her neat rump: "Bonnee."

As for the wives, they were a tight-knit and wary bunch, sitting in the stands afternoon and night, watching their husbands compete and watching the single women through the smoke from their cigarettes. Those that had children left them sleeping in the trailers, and protected their primary interests. Cowboys then, and cowboys now, bear watching.

If the rodeo was in some two-dog town, we might be there for only one daytime and one evening performance, and then it was back on the road again, with a tour of the local bars in between. These had a certain classic similarity—a jukebox playing cowboy songs about lost love and lost illusions, beer signs with neon waterfalls and on the wall the head of a deer with brown glass eyes.

Such bars did not bother to throw kids out, and so we played the pinball machines, or listened to the bragging and the laughter, or put our heads down on the table, among the shot glasses and beer bottles, and slept. Because slot machines were legal in Montana and Nevada, I liked the bars there best; they weren't legal for children, but who was watching? In Helena, Montana, with money I pried loose from my mother by practiced nagging, I won a jackpot. The quarters poured through my hands and onto the floor, a silver river of money.

No one would have thrown me out of the bars whatever I did, because I was Cy Taillon's daughter, his namesake, a miniature version of Cy in my own hand-made boots and my Stetson.

Bartenders served my ginger ale with a cherry in it. Cowboys asked me to dance to the jukebox, and asked Pat if she knew my father had himself another little gal. Expansive on bourbon, Cy sat me on the bar and had me sing "Mexicali Rose." I have no voice, and hadn't then, but what I lacked in musicality, I made up for in volume. I could also imitate my father at the mike, booming out: "The only pay this cowboy is going to get tonight . . ." and other crowd pleasers.

Not only did rodeo people live like gypsies, traveling in an informal caravan from town to town; my father and I looked like gypsies, both dark-skinned to start with and tanned by the sun pounding down on us, both with dark hair and high cheekbones. Mine softened as I grew older. Cy's became more pronounced, until, just before he died, the flesh receded from the bone. Once, when I was ten, and he and I were having lunch in the Florence Hotel in Missoula, Montana, a woman asked to take a snapshot of us. She was from out of town, she said, and we were the first Indians she'd ever seen. We posed for her in front of the Florence's corny Indian murals, palms raised in the B-movie "how" sign.

All of which I took for granted, when our family lived on the road, as the way everyone lived, though a social worker might have taken a dim view of it and I already knew at least one person who did. It was normal to have a dapper, charming father whose public self bore little resemblance to the private Cy, the one who drank too much and flared into an alcohol-fueled temper. It was normal to have a trick-riding, ex-chorus-girl mother who still did dancer's limbering-up exercises every morning, sinking into splits and sitting on the floor spraddle-legged, bending her head first to one knee and then to the other. "You better stay in shape when you grow up," she told me as I watched, "because a woman's looks are all she's got."

It was normal to spend days and nights at the rodeo, listening to Cy's molasses voice and the voices of the cowboys, jawing, swearing and bantering with each other, smelling leather, calves in their pens and horse manure; to sit high above the bleachers in the announcer's stand and all but melt with love and pride when, on cold nights, Cy took his jacket off and put it around me.

It wasn't just normal to live in a Packard, it was classy. A Packard was still a classy car when it was ankle deep in hamburger wrappers. Some rodeo people pulled trailers and thus had the equivalent of houses, but most drove pickups or the kind of cars which, if they were horses, would have been taken off and shot.

I also believed then that Pat would stay spirited and taut-bodied forever, like a young racehorse, and that my father, whenever he wanted to, could make himself invisible. He told me that he could, but not when anybody was watching, and in the somewhat deflected way he always told the truth, he was telling it then.

TWO

A few blocks from my San Francisco apartment, a shop sells high-fashion cowboy boots. Custom-ordered from Texas, in lizard, they cost $1,500. The same shop sells stovepipe jeans to tuck into the boots, sterling and turquoise belt buckles and Ralph Lauren's idea of Western wear.

The shop thrives, though there are no cowboys here, and so do similar shops in Beverly Hills, where on quaintly named Rodeo Drive, one sees pencil-hipped, forever blond TV producers in cowboy regalia, coke spoons dangling from the gold chains around their necks.

The West has been reinterpreted by Clint Eastwood, and nothing is more chic on the hills of San Francisco than a pickup truck. But I worry. Does anyone tell the rhinestone cowboys they'll never get the look right until they have broken every major bone in their bodies? That if they wear needle-toed cowboy boots for long, they'll soon have feet as misshapen as a ballerina's, corn-ridden

appendages that look like tubers and hurt like hell
when the boots come off? That real cowboys don't
wear tinted aviator glasses; they either disappear
behind ink-black lenses or squint into the sun
through eyes red as pickup-truck taillights?

Does anyone warn the owner of a creamy new
Stetson that throwing a cowboy hat on the bed is
bad luck? The next bronc will throw you on the
same shoulder you broke competing in the bareback event in Cheyenne. Your wife will get tired
of watching soap operas on TV, in the motel, while
you're being stuck together with steel pins again,
and leave you, taking the kids, the truck and Bob,
your Aussie dog. Your creditors will close in; many
broken-down bronc riders have few other finely
honed skills except spitting for distance.

Or so it was once. Now some cowboys on the
circuit are MIT graduates or alumni of two years
in Nepal with the Peace Corps. A few are black,
finally staking out their claim on what has until
recently been an all-white segment of mythic
America. San Francisco has a gay rodeo, though
it's not sanctioned by the Professional Rodeo Cowboys Association, and though one brings up the
subject in, say, the Cowboys Bar in Great Falls and
then backs slowly, slowly out the door.

When Cy started out on the circuit, riders were
mostly farm boys like himself, aspiring cowboys
who harassed the horses on the family spread until
they got their big break at Frontier Days in Fargo,
or Waco, or Mandan. Some of them were fifteen
but lied and said they were eighteen, some were

veterans of thirty-five so full of steel by then you
could pick them up with a magnet. Young or old,
after a few lifetimes passed in seconds on the backs
of horses named Powder River or Tailspin Terror,
they walked like arthritic old men. Then as now,
a few died. "Don't worry about it if the ambulance
pulls out of the fairgrounds and the siren is going,"
Cy told me. "You start your worrying when they
don't bother with the siren."

Though rodeo claims a good safety record, compared with other sports and considering the number of participants in it, injuries tend to be
impressive. Horses roll on the riders they've bucked
off, crushing ribs. To drive their point home, they
trample them. Careering around the ring, when a
rider is down, a bronc kicks with the force of a
heavy-gauge shotgun.

Brahma bulls not only gore their fallen riders but
have a knack for finding the soft flesh of the groin.

You can get hurt before you even get out of the
chute, trying to get a saddle on a bronc that crushes
your leg against the chute wall as easily as bending
a straw.

Compared with cowboys, pro football players, in
their helmets and padding, are at no more physical
risk than chess players. So routine are injuries no
one mentions the trivial, the cracked ribs and broken collarbones, and the riders don't cater to them:
when my brother Terry was thrown and got his
teeth rammed through his lower lip years ago,
Tommy mopped up the worst of the blood, packed
Terry's lip with ice and pushed his face back into

something resembling a human face. Terry got on his next horse and rode.

Children are taught to be stoic before they're taught to feed themselves. Get your finger slammed in a car door at the fairgrounds and an embarrassed parent will swoop down on you. "For heaven's sake, will you stop that bawlin'! You can't get yourself in a lather over every whipstitch."

None of which matters, eternally taped ribs or wives clean out of patience, if you love the road. Cy loved it because he was fiercely independent; he'd sooner starve, he said, than work for somebody else. Pat loved it because it led away from Paragould, Arkansas, and poverty. I loved it because it was the life I knew. By my third birthday, I had logged 150,000 miles, occasion for an AP wirephoto captioned: "She Sees America."

It is inaccurate to say we saw America. What we saw was the western half of the country, the straight highways that shimmer in the heat across Nevada and Utah, the small-town fairgrounds where the rodeo was usually part of a country fair or paired up with a carnival. We saw hundreds of cafes called the Stockman's, the Wagon Wheel or the Gold Nugget, all of them serving mashed potatoes with an ice-cream scoop and offering you your choice of dessert, orange sherbet or orange sherbet. We saw hundreds of bars that still set the standard, for me, of a decent place to buy a bourbon-and-branch (in Montana, called a whiskey ditch).

A bar should be cool and dark, a cave hollowed

out of the heat, and it should have a rail, ideally brass, where you can hook your boot heel, the better to settle in and ponder life. The bartender should greet you with "How're you folks today?" and then leave you alone; or if he knows you from other Frontier Days, "Cy, you old son-of-a-gun, how you been keepin'?"

No fake stained glass, no Perrier, and if the bar serves food, no friendly-puppy waiters crying, "Hi! My name is Roger. I'm your serving person tonight."

A decent bar will produce a napkin for a lady, one with cheerfully crass cartoons on it, possibly the only napkin in the place. The cartoons will feature steatopygic women wearing no underpants and surprised by a high wind. Caption: "Just Bummin' Around."

There should be the summer smell of beer sprinkled with salt, the pleasant reek of sour mash bourbon, a rack with Planters peanuts in bags you have to rip open with your teeth, another rack with nail clippers and one with key chains: "Souvenir of Puyallup, Washington." A waitress is optional, but if there is one, her name should be Velma.

Walk out of such a bar on a hot day, into the glare of the street, open the doors of your car, with its melting tires, and you'll get an idea of what it's like to burn in hell.

These are some of the big-time rodeos Cy announced year after year: the Rodeo de Santa Fe, Santa Fe, New Mexico; the Snake River Stampede, Nampa, Idaho; the Pike's Peak or Bust Rodeo,

Colorado Springs, Colorado; the Southwestern Exposition and Rodeo, Fort Worth, Texas; the Canadian Western Stock Show and Rodeo, Edmonton, Alberta. The small-time ones all took place, in my memory, in the same smoldering town with a ratty arena and a bar called The Last Roundup.

From the Black Hills Roundup in Belle Fourche, South Dakota, most years, we went to Cavalier, North Dakota, just across the border from Manitoba, and the farm where my father grew up. His father, Eli Taillon, and his mother, the first white child to be born in Pembina County and the former Philomine Dumas, still lived there. Born in 1870, she lived to be eighty-seven and left twenty-one great-grandchildren. Until my generation, it was a good Catholic family.

A tiny woman, Grandma Taillon still made her own lye soap in a boiling kettle in the yard; refused to "hook up to the electricity," so that the farmhouse, at night, swam in the shadows cast by kerosene lamps; killed chickens with fearsome skill. Preparing for Sunday dinner, she grabbed a hen by the neck and swung it in circles until its neck and its will to live gave out. Shrieks and the beating of wings and the figure of my grandmother, upright and still except for her implacably whirring arm. I tried to behave myself at her house.

Of Cy's nine brothers and sisters, all but two had left the farm and its backbreaking days. Uncle Henry worked it, and Aunt Ida, ageless in her great bulk, presided over the kitchen. A sea beast thrown

up on land, Ida wore dresses the size of tents, made
of printed sacking, and bedroom slippers with the
tops of the toes cut out. Though she made shy
overtures to me, I thought of her as made of the
same dough as the bread she baked every day, soft,
white and repulsive, and hurt her feelings by whin-
ing for store bread instead. Child of the truck stops,
I hated farm food, especially those all too fresh
chickens, and longed for french fries cooked in
rancid grease.

We never stayed in Cavalier more than a few
days. Pat was bored before the car came to a stop
in front of the house, feeling correctly that she was
out of place there. A woman who never could master the swivel-handled potato peeler, she had nothing to contribute in the way of usefulness, and no
one called on her to rattle out a barrage of tap
steps or do splits up a wall. Nor did anyone else
on the farm own a fitted cosmetics case or wear
white lounging pajamas. Grandma Taillon and Ida
knew nothing about either lip brushes or lounging.

"Go talk to Ida, damn it," Cy said when Pat
complained. She and I exchanged horrified looks.

Thirty years later I became curious about Ida,
but she was dead and it was too late to ask her why
she never left home, never married, spent her own
eighty-seven years at the pump handle and over
the wood stove. I am left with her obituary and
what it reveals about her lifetime of duty and hard
work: charter member of the Tongue River Home-
makers Club; 4-H leader; member of the Tongue
River Sewing Circle, the American Legion Auxil-

iary, the Pembina County Pioneer Daughters, St. Bridget's Catholic Church and its Altar Society.

A patchwork quilt she made for us tells the same plain tale. With twenty varieties of fancy stitch, none repeated in the whole, the quilt is the work of a woman who loved her needle. But it's meant for utility, not beauty. The odd-shaped pieces of fabric are homely, cut from the sleeve of a worn cotton work shirt, a pair of whipcord pants or a flannel shirt. How Ida must have longed to cut just one sleeve off one of my mother's silk blouses or one cuff off her bell-bottomed satin pants, to feel the slippery stuff under her needle.

Pat and I were both outsiders on the farm because the language spoken there was mostly Canadian French. Cy spoke it. We neither spoke nor understood it. Much of the time, during those visits, Cy was hidden away, helping my grandmother take care of his father.

Grandfather Taillon was nearly deaf. All communication with him took place by shouting in French, and since he rarely came out of his downstairs room, from which there issued forth bellows and thumps, I thought he was mad. In several visits to Elm Croft, the farm's name, I saw him only a few times, a gaunt old man with Cy's strong cheekbones, yellowed gray hair and hawk's eyes. Though he spoke to me kindly, if unintelligibly, Cy quickly took him back to his room, seeming embarrassed by him and shooing him down the dark hall with what sounded like threats and invective. I think he must have wanted me to think of my grandfather as a gentleman landowner instead of a wild-looking old man, an apparition in long underwear.

Always, Cy's pattern was to treat things as grander than they were, as if the reality would compromise him. When he made me a gift of his ordinary violin many years later—or rather lent it to me, because he soon took it back—he insisted that it was a Stradivarius.

Nonetheless, he loved Elm Croft and the Red River valley in which it was situated, the flat, loamy fields surrounded by woods, the swimming hole with its heart-stopping rope swing and the farm animals, especially the horses.

Mechanization came late to the farm, and its horses were working animals that pulled threshers and bundle wagons for the haying. When Cy was growing up they also pulled the buggy, the light cutter, the sleigh and the Taillon brothers, who skied the frozen ditches in the winter, towed along at bone-rattling speed behind Old Ned, Cy's favorite. Ned, he wrote in an article called "Once a Farm Boy," was a roan weighing 1,250 pounds, "of uncertain lineage, with some Percheron blood."

In the same piece, he writes about the life of the place, the grueling hard work, the rosary his mother recited every night in French, with the family and the neighbors kneeling around her, and the joys of informal evening musicales. The family had its own orchestra of self-taught musicians, with all the children playing instruments—"fiddles, guitars, piano, xylophone, auto-harp, trumpet and drums"—except for Ida. She never learned to play, Cy notes, because she was too burdened with cooking and housekeeping chores.

With the other Taillon boys, he fished in the neighboring streams, hunted in the woods for bush rabbits, partridges and coyotes and ice-skated on the frozen Tongue River in the winters, when the temperatures dropped as low as sixty below zero. He played his fiddle and acted as a caller for square dances in farmhouses "where the musicians would usually stand in a doorway between two rooms filled with sweating and stomping revelers."

Elm Croft couldn't hold him. How can you keep a boy like Cy down on the farm after he's seen Fargo? But it formed him, so that the farm boy remained even when a reporter was describing him as "blasé and full of adjectives as a circus advance man." Resplendent in a satin Western shirt, boots and cowboy hat, on one of those visits he once took me out to the barn, where a colt had just been born. He had me smell its breath. "Sweet as new hay," he said. "Sweet as a baby's."

Yet he seemed happy to have left the place when we were back on the road again, with the world framed by the windshield. Shaking the dust of Cavalier off his feet, Cy merely traded it for different dust, but for him the dust of the rodeo arena was like greasepaint for actors. It had seeped through his skin; he missed it painfully when we were away long. In the winters, when there were no rodeos, he drank with more determination, got into more trouble—the infinite varieties of it having to do with money and women—and was dangerous to be near, volatile and looking for a fight. His restlessness was that of a bucking horse in the chute. My mother's mood wasn't markedly better.

A former chanteuse, as well as the tap-dancing sensation of St. Louis, Pat had a throaty contralto voice. She had no range at all but could have turned "Onward, Christian Soldiers" into a torch song. I remember her singing "Don't Fence Me In" along with the radio. "Let me ride thru the wide-open country that I love . . . Don't fence me in."

It could have been their theme song. I made the back seat of the car into a nest and filled it full of clothes, books, blankets and my collections: matchbooks, bar napkins, rodeo programs and swizzle sticks. They left laundry in towns all over the circuit because they were too impatient to wait for it to be ready; threw the windows and the door open when we slept in motor court cabins, to let in fresh air and cowboys looking for a place to bunk; seemed to think walls and a ceiling would cave in and smother them; rarely made it all the way through a movie. "Come on, now." My mother dragged me up the aisle, still riveted to Yvonne De Carlo, and out of the theater. "I can't stand to stay cooped up in this place."

Somebody usually picked up the laundry anyway, settled our bar bill and paid off the irate owner of the Drop Inn when we left his motor court at dawn, ahead of schedule and the bill. Film crews have retinues who follow them on location, sweeping up rubble and settling damage claims. Cy and Pat attracted a retinue of their own, loners drawn to them as a glamorous couple and admirers who saw themselves reflected in their high shine.

It was a thankless job, in their case. They didn't really care about bills and laundry or about orderly lives. But for the most patient of the loners, it eventually paid off.

Meanwhile we rolled along in the Packard, hell-bent for Dallas, Fort Worth, Baton Rouge and Alabama City. We had our classy car, and gas money. We could sing three-part harmony to "San Antonio Rose." We had the Brahma bull by the tail.

THREE

~~~~~~

My mother once told a friend why she left Paragould, Arkansas. "I got tired of grits." Paragould
is poultry-raising country. Cold in the winters, it
swelters in the summertime. A few years ago, a
Deep South heat wave killed off the chickens by
the thousands. An Arkansas cousin wrote that they
were "keeling right over, already roasted," while
in Little Rock, nearby, that same summer, one man
shot and killed another over holes made in a plastic wading pool.

At sixteen, Nedra Ann Montgomery fled the cli-
mate and the cuisine and departed Arkansas for
St. Louis, where she changed her name to Patricia.
"Pat Montgomery" would look better on a mar-
quee. Her mother, Minnie Mae, had died of tuber-
culosis at forty-five, leaving "Baby Sister" in the
care of her older sisters, Lucille, Hester, Cleo and
Ila Mae. A brother, Rudolph, was in reform school.
Their father, Brown Montgomery, was the town

drunk and, according to another cousin, Clifton, "mean as a weasel."

Brown was the engineer for the city waterworks. Widowed, he spent his time drinking corn whiskey, tending the boiler at the Paragould power plant and shooting at anything that moved, including Clifton. As a child, Clifton was dispatched to fetch Brown home for Sunday dinner. He remembers with clarity a discussion between them punctuated with blasts from a 12-gauge shotgun.

Because Brown had once been a railroad man, his children could ride the trains on free passes. Nedra Ann got on the train in Paragould, with no one's permission, no profession and no prospects, and got off in St. Louis reborn as Pat Montgomery, dancer and singer; or, as she preferred to call herself, "soubrette."

The next sister up the line, Ila Mae, never forgave her. "Oh no, Baby Sister couldn't settle for honest work as a fry cook."

My mother had always danced, Ila Mae told me in our last conversation before she died. My aunt made it clear she hadn't changed her views on the subject of life upon the stage. "She used to get on an old box, or a tub, or anything she could, and just dance her head off. And she'd say, 'Someday they're going to have to pay to see me.' My brother would laugh, and she'd say, 'Gimme some pennies.' Well, they didn't have one penny between them, you know. But there she was, dancing on some old box out in the backyard like a fool."

Pat got a job modeling for a department store

and found work at night as a chorus girl in a less prestigious theater across the street from St. Louis's finest, the Fox. But she had lean times at first, and I suppose she lived then the way poor girls like her have always lived when they came to the city, that she found a man, or men, to serve as her protector while she took her bearings. Souvenirs of her St. Louis days were still among the thin rag endings of her personal possessions thirty years later: a carnelian dinner ring hidden in the back of a drawer, a note reading "After the show, I sure do hate to wait!," a papery pressed gardenia.

Whatever she found in St. Louis, and despite Ila Mae's having followed her there to keep a custodial eye upon her, she didn't go home to Paragould for years, not until she could go back in style. Nor did she attend her father's funeral when he died, widely unmourned. Brown had remarried. His sixteen-year-old second wife had buck teeth. Brown tormented her by telling everyone that Lily could eat an apple through a knothole.

Because Pat was five feet two, she was a "pony," the shortest dancer in a chorus line and the one positioned at the end. She caught the attention of the Fox Theater management anyway and soon moved across the street to its glittering variety show. Vaudeville was flourishing in the mid-twenties. The Fox, Ila Mae recalled, was "really a high-class place, with a big orchestra pit down below, and the orchestra would rise up on a platform. They had all these gorgeous costumes, and beautiful music, and comedy, tap dancing . . ."

Soon the Fox featured Miss Pat Montgomery—
"And Can She Sing and Tap!"—as female lead.
Cousin Clifton, twelve years old then, rode the
magic train to St. Louis, with his mother, to see
my mother perform. At the end of her big solo
number, the audience pelted her with bouquets.
Said Clifton, remembering, "I swear, I thought it
was raining roses."

In rapid order, her star on the rise, Pat audi-
tioned as a singer with the Municipal Opera, was
hired and became "specialty featured artist." She
joined the Missouri Theater's Missouri Rockets—
"One of the Finest, Most Versatile Choruses to
Ever Set Foot Behind Footlights." She went off to
New York with Ernie Young's Revue in the chorus
of a production called *Rain or Shine*.

The Revue didn't dazzle New York, but my
mother was there long enough to antagonize her
four sisters, who thought it was time she settled
down, by sending them a postcard: "Have hit the
big time." The others were all sensibly married by
their late teens, and all were devoted to grits. Only
Ila Mae had pursued a career—as a fry cook.

Like Cy, Pat invented herself, with energy and
imagination. She rapidly learned to wear stylish
clothes, lost her Arkansas accent and became expert at cosmetics. When she finished working with
her sable brushes, her pots and jars and hand mirror, her thin upper lip was the top half of a heart,
her eyebrows two horizontal commas. Her own
eyebrows, she banished, to conform to an ideal of
beauty. If thine eyebrow offend thee, pluck it out.

Vain beyond common sense, she thought her size 7 feet were too large and crammed them into size 5½ shoes. I have seen her cry because they hurt so much by the end of an evening, and I have seen Cy pick her up in his arms and carry her to the Packard, wobbling on the high heels of his cowboy boots. It wouldn't have occurred to either of them that Pat could take her shoes off, not when they flattered her ankles and made her look taller, and it wouldn't have occurred to me, either. I shared my parents' highly developed sense of what is important.

Pat was so consistent about this that her scrapbook, like my father's, is a patchy record of her career. She clipped and pasted as selectively as he did and even scratched out other faces in photos. Why should she read about or look at photos of anyone but herself?

What evidence that more or less survived shows that she danced at Billy Rose's Golden Horseshoe, having moved on to conquer Chicago, as well as less glamorous nightclubs. These have names such as the Four Aces (with its Famous Four Ace Band of Rhythm) and the Golden Pumpkin, "The Most Beautiful Chinese Cafe in the World." Signing on with Ernie Young again, she played the Oriental Village at the Chicago World's Fair, where, for reasons that cannot be reconstructed, the group elected to perform something called *Spanish Nights*. The Revue also played the provinces.

A snapshot on which she wrote "My Al, Minot, North Dakota, 1931" preserves the flavor of those tours. A dusty Plymouth sits in a field, with a line of sagging tents in the background. On the Plymouth is a placard: "Ernie Young's Productions, Featuring Al Reynolds, Chicago's Favorite Son. 50 PEOPLE!" "My Al" leans on the car, looking jaunty in a sport coat, impeccable white shirt and pale striped pants. In front of that tent city in a field, he's dressed for Ascot.

"Always kicking!" reads the caption on another snapshot, this one of my mother braced against a telephone pole in the middle of nowhere, showing off her extension. In still another, she does splits at the top of a flagpole. Caption: "Was it shaky up here? Oh boy & how!" Her good cheer seems unflappable, even when she's waving around in a high wind.

Then she met Cy Taillon, and after a twenty-four-hour courtship, married him. They must have looked at each other and instantly recognized their similarities: two peacocks in a world of mud hens.

Cy was announcing the 1931 Montana State Fair, in Great Falls. Pat was part of the featured entertainment, Ernie Young's road company. The tour was a vacation, she told reporters, before she went off to a starring engagement on Broadway. Enthralled, the Great Falls paper printed her picture, Cy's picture and the headline: "Radio Announcer Weds Revue Girl."

In St. Louis, Ila Mae got a telegram. "She didn't explain anything, just said they were married and that was it. My brother Rudy said, 'Oh my God, a radio man. They're as bad as actors. She'll never settle down, she'll dance and dance the rest of her life.' " Ila Mae wired back: "Baby Sister and Cy, Good luck."

They needed it, because as the best man at their wedding later observed, with unconcealed satisfaction, "they didn't have enough sense between them for a good plow horse."

I have said my parents attracted a retinue, people drawn to their specious glamour; they seemed to give off light, noise and gaiety, like a house in which there is a perpetual party going on, and people gravitated to them and stayed. The one who stayed longest was Roy Qualley, my father's friend and self-appointed caretaker.

Eleven years older than Cy, Roy was also from a big family and a farm, this one in Decorah, Iowa. In old photos, the farmhouse springs out of the flat expanse surrounding it like some strange outcropping. Unsoftened by a single tree, a sprawling carpenter gothic house high off the ground on its foundation, it looks like a model made of cardboard.

Roy's grandparents immigrated from Norway, changing the spelling of their name. Kvale became Qualley. In photos, the family is unsmiling; they all have Roy's stolid, level gaze, parents and children alike looking resigned to hard work, the monotonous midwestern landscape and virtue as its own reward. While they shared little in terms of temperament, Roy and Cy shared a common background and the urge to escape from it.

Roy's nickname was Old Honest Face. It was he

who paid the bar bills, extricated my hot-tempered, bantamweight father from fistfights and saw that Cy made it to the radio station most mornings. Square and stocky, already balding by the time he reached his twenties, he had delivered newspapers in Great Falls, sold encyclopedias door to door in Spokane and mined gold in the hills above Helena.

A lifelong self-improver, he clipped from a 1927 Spokane newspaper Mussolini's Efficiency Precepts:

> Master your body and mind.
> Concentrate on the one thing before you.
> Get seven hours' sound sleep.
> Never stay in bed after the instant of
>   awakening.
> Read the newspapers while dressing.
> Shave: I am anti-whiskers.
> Drink a glass of milk for breakfast.

The lure of gold brought Roy out West, and once, he struck it. With a partner, he hit what was reported as "an important strike of high-grade gold ore," but something went wrong and the mine and the dream got away. Undaunted, he staked out another claim and clipped another newspaper story that must have held out promise to him: "In His Prison Cell, Convict Turns Sand into Gold — The Secret of the Medieval Alchemists Rediscovered."

Ila Mae thought Cy and Roy met in some Great Falls boardinghouse. Both lived in numbers of them, old houses converted into hotels and catering to single men. She also thought Cy invested in one of Roy's mining ventures, though money, as Roy liked to say, burned a hole in Cy's pocket. He invested it mainly in goodwill. However the connection developed, they were tightly if oddly linked.

Roy worked out on barbells at the YMCA. He took business school correspondence courses and read books on nutrition and hair growth. Cy drank, caroused and still had more hair than he needed.

Roy saved every receipt. Cy was thirty-five before he had a bank account.

Roy said severely that all Cy thought you could buy with money was a good time. Cy said of Roy, "He tried to keep me on the straight and narrow path, and I did his fast living for him. He got to hear about it, and it saved him a lot of money and the wear and tear on his physique."

Theirs was a reciprocal exchange, and when my mother came along, she got Roy as part of the package, inscribing a photo of herself, wearing clinging silk and an ankle bracelet: "To Roy, the Best Pal in the World." Now Roy had not only my father to keep on the straight and narrow but also Pat, who showed a cheerful preference for the wide and convoluted.

He must have liked the amplified job duties. Like Ila Mae, Roy was a born heel snapper, one of the sheep dogs among us who like to nip at other people's ankles and herd them into line. In another throwback to early conditioning, I can recognize a heel snapper on sight, in or out of uniform, with or without brass buttons.

"Somebody has to do it," such people generally defend themselves. In this instance, Roy was right. Put two careless people together, and the damage increases disproportionately—more debts, more broken glass and more threats of lawsuits for alienation of affections. When Leo Cremer, a big, benign man known as a steady hand with horses, contracted with my father to announce rodeos for him, he tried to get my parents to stop doing their imitation of Scott and Zelda. But the life of the circuit, which Pat embraced enthusiastically, didn't help. Unlike their Rodeo Drive imitators, tall in the saddles of their Mercedes, real rodeo cowboys aren't known for their consumption of white wine and soda.

Rocketing along from rodeo to rodeo, Pat and Cy drove the car they owned before the Packard, a Ford sedan painted yellow. Always, they posed with it in the background of snapshots, the way another couple might have posed on their front porch.

Tireless in her efforts to rehabilitate my mother, Ila Mae had moved from Arkansas to Great Falls to be near them. Now she teamed up with Roy in disapproving mightily of their lives. Perhaps because she was unofficial title holder for world's cleanest woman, she wasn't taken with their style of traveling. "You should have seen that car of theirs. It was *filthy*, and that yellow color showed up every speck of dirt. All those clothes of theirs were stuffed in the back, piled right up to the ceiling. They couldn't be bothered with suitcases, they just threw everything they owned in the back seat and went off. Pat drove if Cy was drunk, and she drove like a cowboy, or a maniac." To Ila Mae, the two were one and the same.

She was bitter about life in general. Her husband had run off with another woman, who caught his eye over the grave at a funeral. She'd lost her only child in infancy. There she was, working as a waitress, thirty years old and secondhand goods. Men were lustful beasts, and it didn't improve her state of mind that Baby Sister cottoned to the creatures. "Pat, or whatever you call yourself now," she wrote, in care of Rodeo Headquarters, Deer Lodge, Montana, "always remember our body is a Temple and God means for us to keep it sweet and clean. You showed it off on the stage all those years, *that's enough*."

From her account of my parents, and cousin Clifton's, I see the six years of their marriage before I was born as a frenetic silent movie—the yellow Ford smoking out of some small town, with creditors, love-stricken saddle-bronc riders and faithful Roy Qualley in pursuit; loud quarrels and impassioned reconciliations; a supporting cast of Other Women, Other Men. Pat and Cy competed in sexual conquest as they competed in everything else.

Two small people with enormous egos, they loved each other but needed the reassurance to be found in numbers, the proof that marriage hadn't dimmed their separate luster. When Cy parked Pat on the farm in North Dakota one summer, the better to cut his own wide swath on the circuit, she seduced every able-bodied man for miles. "The only thing you told me not to do," she drawled at Cy when he came back to get her, summoned by his mother, "was smoke in the barn."

Says another cousin, also visiting the farm that summer, "That girl was a living fireball."

Briefly, after this episode, my parents made an attempt at conventional domesticity. They set up a small apartment in Billings, Montana, where Pat kept house and cooked dinners Cy rarely came home at night to eat. He was flying small planes again, too restless to remain earthbound.

Pat teamed up with a male dancer and opened a dance studio. It became a huge success. But it closed a few months after it opened. "Some jealousy developed between Cy and her business partner," Ila Mae said discreetly. "I don't remember just what it was all about." Pat gave up both the apartment and the studio and joined Cy on the road.

Ila Mae had married again, to a gentle, round-faced clothing salesman named Wiley Gosney, and also moved West. Their own apartment in Great Falls became my parents' mail drop and the place where they bunked when they weren't on the road.

This proved a trial for Ila Mae. She could lecture my mother about cleanliness and its proximity to godliness, and how "undies worn twice aren't very nice." The two couples could share expenses.

But Cy tended to disappear for two or three days at a time, coming home when the poker game finally wound down, and docile Wiley, who stayed good-humored even when told to wash his hands ten times a day, was in Ila Mae's view too sorry for Pat and too ready with his ironed, starched handkerchief. Pat became pregnant. Ila Mae had a good reason to ask that they find a place of their own.

Unlikely candidates for parenthood, Cy and Pat made the best of it. They took two rooms in a boardinghouse, with the second for a nursery. I was born, another newsworthy event to the Great Falls *Tribune*. They started a scrapbook for me. Scrapbooks, in my family, are a way of life. You may have nothing else, but you've got your press clippings.

In two weeks, we were on the road again. Where Cy went, Pat was going, with or without a baby. Either she knew better, by now, than to send him off on his own, or he knew enough to insist that she come with him.

Soon I was big enough to be outfitted like a Western Barbie doll and had a role in their long-playing drama. I played what my mother called Little Pat and Cy called Little Cyra and my aunt called "the poor little thing."

And I had a glorious time, as unofficial mascot of the rodeo, from Canada to New Mexico, though my parents sometimes forgot momentarily that I existed. After a long night larking in the bars in Cheyenne, Wyoming, they once left me sleeping in a motor court bed, packed up and headed for the next rodeo. Seventy miles out of town, they had to turn around and go back.

"The poor little thing needs regular hours and good food & training," Ila Mae wrote, in letters that sometimes tracked us down weeks after they were written. Sometimes I stayed with her for a few weeks or a month and got all three of these things, as well as scrubbed inhumanly clean. They held little appeal for me. Mild Wiley watched me chafe under her regime and sometimes intervened. "For Chrissake, let the kid wear her cowboy hat." He only got us both in trouble.

Cy Taillon.

Cyra.

Cy and Pat Taillon in the early years of their marriage.

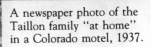

A newspaper photo of the Taillon family "at home" in a Colorado motel, 1937.

Cyra in cowboy gear at about age two.

The "golden-voiced" Cy at the mike.

An early publicity photo of Pat.

Al Reynolds of Ernie Young's Revue, 1931.

always Kicking!
Ernie young
reaha

Helena
mont.

Pat on the road in
Helena, Montana, 1931.

*Was it shaky up here
oh boy & how.* Helena m
1931

The daily dozen — Pat.
Helena
mont.

Pat as a young chanteuse.

Ila Mae at about eighteen.

A newly married Ila Mae with her second husband, Wiley Gosney.

Cyra at the time she was considered the unofficial mascot of the rodeo circuit.

FOUR

"One time I came home, and here was boots and saddles and everything else on the sun porch, and you were in my bed, and Cy and Pat had took off again." At seventy-five, Ila Mae sounded as irate, despite the intervening years, as she must have that afternoon in 1940 or so. The problem with Baby Sister, she said, was that she'd never had proper training herself. "The older girls wouldn't let her do anything. I did it. I stood on a box and made pies."

When my mother stood on a box, she danced, and I doubt that her motherless childhood had much to do with it. No one was less suited to pie baking. On the rare occasions when we had a room with a kitchenette and Pat cooked, the food was inedible. Food didn't interest my mother. She'd have preferred to take a pill in order to stay nourished and not waste time better spent kicking up her heels.

If she sewed a button on a shirt for Cy, she stuck

herself with the needle and bled on it. She was a copious bleeder.

Refusing to learn the right way to pull a cowboy's boots off for him, she faced Cy and tugged, instead of standing with her back to him and straddling his outstretched leg. He swore. Pat rocked his foot back and forth in her hands and swore back at him. When the boot came off, she hurtled across the room, caught up in the momentum.

She was a soubrette, not a housewife, and if Cy sometimes forgot it, Pat never did. In our household, what mattered was style, not substance.

They were passionate about clothes, both of them. Pat had a fur coat, made of beaver tails and known as her mink, and dozens of hats that I loved to try on. She claimed that her swirling, bright dresses were made in Paris, France. On the road, in the heat, she wore high-heeled shoes that showed off her legs and wide-legged shorts. In her wardrobe, there were no pastels; she saw life, and herself, in primary colors.

So did Cy, who customarily wore satin and sateen shirts in the colors of parrot feathers, narrow-legged Western pants and the fanciest boots he could find. Straight out of bed in the morning, he pulled them on. He looked peculiar, since he slept in shorts and undershirt, but with his boots on, he was nine feet tall in his own eyes and in mine. It took me twenty years to realize my father was a small man.

Shoes hurt his feet. He owned a pair of black cowboy boots for funerals.

Not left out of all this sartorial splendor, I had my own black felt cowboy hat with white trim and a chin strap, gabardine pants and plaid shirts, neckerchiefs with silver slides and my own tooled boots, the first pair I owned a few inches long. Years later, Cy had these bronzed for me. They came back from the mail-order house that turned them into bookends with a printed card enclosed: "Baby's First Shoes."

How and if these clothes were ever paid for, I don't know. On one desperate occasion, when we needed gas and had no money, we pulled into a one-pump gas station and filled up. Coached by my parents, I used the bathroom, stayed in for a while as a diversionary tactic, then bolted out and jumped on the running board of the already moving Packard. We must not have paid for the gas, because the red-faced attendant ran after us for a short distance, yelling at us.

I suppose my mother's finery was left over from her chorus girl days, a kind of dowry. Cy must have purchased his with charm and credit.

Nor do I know how they paid for all the studio photographs they had taken, recording for posterity the latest additions to our wardrobes. Though Roy said money burned a hole in Cy's pocket, it rarely traveled that far between his hand and the bar. Pat was a two-fisted drinker. Cy was a drunk, charming and good-humored when sober, combative and cold-eyed when full of bourbon.

Their fights began to heat up. Her makeup case on her lap, Pat sat in the passenger seat of the

Packard, spitting on a sponge and putting pancake makeup on her black eyes. She'd banged herself up, she told me, bumping into something in the dark.

Those fights were the private side of their lives together. Cy disappeared and reappeared, when we were anywhere as long as a few days, throwing the door of a room open late at night with a bang that woke me and set my heart racing with anticipation. They shouted at each other until Pat hurled herself at Cy like a terrier. They wrestled, lurching back and forth across the room in a parody of the way they danced, bodies locked together. Before I learned not to intervene, I wrapped myself around Cy's pant leg. He reached for his belt buckle.

Belt buckles the size of salad plates are cowboy fetishes. Gold, silver or both, they are awarded as prizes in major rodeos and put up as security for loans. When Cy took off his belt, I knew he was going to use it on my backside, but matters rarely reached that point. All he had to do to reduce me to whimpering panic was reach for the buckle.

When the fight was over and we were all in bed, I heard Cy crying. He was trying to do something, he told my mother, about his "complex."

It wasn't pride alone that kept Pat from cutting and running. She loved Cy with the kind of love that motivates kamikaze pilots. As much as they fought, whittled away at each other's egos and competed for the limelight, they took fierce pride in their respective prizes: the fireball of a woman who stood on the stage in a rainstorm of roses, the darkly handsome man other men liked and other women pursued.

They had a child, for whose affection they also competed. Behind their surface glamour, they were equally insecure. Cy still had to scratch for engagements. Pat had come home from her last tour with a dance company with her tail between her legs. Having ridden the bus nonstop from New York to Great Falls, she ended up on Ila Mae's doorstep. "Half dead, and the dirt beneath her fingernails. I said to her, just wash your hands and go to bed. She must have slept for two, three days."

Between them, they owned a car, not yet paid for, their clothes and a couple of saddles. Together they stood, however shakily, and divided they fell. So they made up their quarrels in bed, and in the morning faced the world again over a table in some coffee shop, joking with the waitress and ordering French toast for me as a signal that the good times were beginning again.

In the car, to get back in my good graces, Cy turned into an affectionate father and a good buddy again, instructing me on the finer points of rodeo: how it was the only authentically American sport. How cowboys had to be tougher than any other athletes. "Put a football player on one of Leo's bucking horses, and there wouldn't be enough left of him to send home to his poor old mother." Why Brahma-bull riders should be small. "They're like jockeys. They've got to be light, because the bigger the man, the slower the reflexes." How misguided it was of outsiders to think the sport was cruel, an attitude that rankled my father all his life.

Bucking horses were born to buck. They liked nothing better than the chance to make some cowboy wish he'd gone into selling insurance. Why weren't the bleeding hearts worried about the riders?

The silver and honey voice spoke only to me, and I forgot the night before and began to think about the next rodeo. If there was a carnival playing the same fairgrounds, Cy would toss me a long strip of free tickets. He had connections. I spent some of the best evenings of my life riding Ferris wheels.

Less happily, we might arrive in town to find "Uncle Roy" Qualley waiting for us. Working a mining claim when he wasn't traveling as a salesman, Roy wasn't in tandem with us as often anymore, but his relationship to our family confused me anyway. I knew Ila Mae was married to Wiley. I still thought of her as married to Roy. It had something to do with their parallel world views.

"Leave the baby with me if you're going to go chasing around the countryside forever," Ila Mae kept urging my parents. Her strong card was my health. I had "spells" of vomiting, was too thin, with sharp knees and sharper collarbones, and couldn't gain weight. I needed liver, spinach and homemade rolls.

Roy was shy with me and issued no edicts about my upbringing, but he doled out dimes and quarters and weeks later expressed dismay that I hadn't saved them. A penny saved was a penny earned. From little acorns mighty oaks grow. He held no brief for investing your capital in slot machines.

Aware that I had to start school soon somewhere, I was afraid Ila Mae would prevail. The last time I'd stayed with her, she'd stripped me naked on the front porch of her apartment building when I came in from the yard, so I wouldn't track dirt into the house. The phrase didn't exist then, but I still consider this child abuse.

That summer started out as another freewheeling season on the circuit. Between rodeos, to keep body and soul together, Cy announced air shows and amateur nights in small-town movie theaters, did some carnival barking—as a personal favor, he explained, to one of the carnies, who was also French Canadian—and took us to Leo Cremer's ranch in Big Timber, Montana, where we rode, fished and played poker. For a few weeks, we lived with a couple named Pearl and Earl in a Billings boardinghouse, which had a resident German shepherd and was generous with the raisins in the tapioca. When we bought a small trailer, no bigger than a pup tent, I knew the purchase meant we were prospering.

Cy told people that he had a "handle on my complex." He wasn't drinking for weeks at a time, intervals when my mother also stopped singing "Stormy Weather" endlessly, her theme song when she had a radio program in St. Louis. They were talking about settling down in Billings for part of the year; I could start school, Cy would work in radio again and Pat would open another Studio of the Dance. Cy said she might be too out of shape. Pat slid into vertical splits up the side of a door frame to prove she wasn't, one of her more startling acrobatic feats.

But she wasn't always kicking that summer, her feistiness intact but her physical vitality dimmed. Afternoons, she lay in bed with a wet washcloth on her forehead, complaining of headaches. Ila Mae rode the bus to Billings and conferred with Cy behind closed doors. The two voices rose and tangled, while I pushed my statues of horses around, in the next room, and tried to eavesdrop.

After one of these conferences, Cy stalked past me, announcing that he was on his way to get drunk. "Poor little thing," Ila Mae said, following on his heels and gathering me into her arms. For something productive to do, she took me off to the bathroom and attacked the skin on my elbows with a pumice stone.

Pat was the beauty of the five Montgomery girls, though studying her photographs, I cannot tell how much of her beauty was nature and how much art. While Ila Mae was also small, dark and vivid, her prettiness was sharp-edged, her animation born of nervous energy. She washed. She sewed, turning out the drab dresses neither my mother nor I ever wore, made of "goods" that would last longer than either of us. She put up jams and jellies, stored winter clothes in mothballs and, in the spring, hung them out on clotheslines to air. She sat me down and taught me how to hem tea towels in neat little whipstitches, though I proved to be a bleeder like my mother, and though no matter how neatly I sewed, Ila Mae ripped the hems out and made me do them over again.

Idle hands were the devil's work, she said, and took on the job of my religious education, also neglected. I had to learn to love Jesus, who had died for my sins.

A picture called "The Sacred Heart" hung in Ila Mae's spare bedroom, over the bed I slept in when I visited her—Jesus with reproachful brown eyes, chest open at the sternum, and his exposed heart dripping a single drop of blood. The Sacred Heart gave me nightmares, though it was intended to inspire me to right living and piety, and I threw tantrums over sleeping in the same room with it. "About Cyra's disposition hope it has improved for she has plenty of room," noted one of Ila Mae's letters.

Doctors came to the boardinghouse, carrying black bags, attended Pat, and then drew blood samples from me. She had the headaches. I got stuck with the needles and resented it. The summer that began so promisingly was fading into confusion, tension and the misery of staying in one place for weeks at a time. Ila Mae came and went, telling me to keep my voice down, stay out from underfoot and pray for improvements of my character. God knew everything I did. *Everything.* Not a sparrow falleth, nor a child with a smart mouth on her sass her aunt.

Cy came and went, drunk as often as he was sober. Pat came and went. Despite orders to stay in bed, she got dressed, put on her makeup, pulled a cloche hat over her spit curls and went dancing with Pinky, a friend from the old days. They were going down to the Club, they said, for a little fun and a Chicken Snack. While Pat dressed, Pinky sat on the bed and sang for me "I Don't Want to Set the World on Fire."

Pinky had pink cheeks, pink clothes and pink cotton candy hair. Ila Mae said she wasn't any better than she should be.

Toward the end of the summer, Cy got the first two-day rodeo he'd been hired for all summer, somewhere in eastern Montana. Pat and I went with him. The second night, because I caught "walking pneumonia," we had to go back to Billings. There my parents had their last fight, probably exacerbated by their worries about money.

I watched it from the distance imposed by a high fever, not greatly alarmed. They always fought; they always made up; they were a matched pair, like two pintos with similar markings. The fight took place in the trailer, and I watched with detachment the steps of their familiar, intricate dance.

I fell asleep. In the morning, Cy was gone and my mother was still dressed. She looked at me with the same detachment I had felt the night before and began to rummage in the mess she and Cy had made of the trailer, digging for my jacket. We were going to see Pearl and Earl, she said, so she could use the telephone in the boardinghouse.

Privately as well as publicly, Cy's every gesture had flair. Liberating himself from Pat and the wreck of their marriage that night, he unhitched the trailer from the Packard and drove away. He'd "gotten hitched." Now he got unhitched.

Pat made her phone call, and the following day, Roy Qualley came to Billings and performed an act just as tidily symbolic. With the trailer hitch he had brought along, he attached our house on wheels to his own car and hauled us away.

FIVE

〰〰〰〰〰〰〰〰〰〰〰〰〰〰〰〰〰〰〰〰〰〰〰〰〰

Thus began the next phase of Pat's life, and Cy's, and my introduction to normal living, as opposed to traipsing around on the rodeo circuit. Roy had been in love with my mother for twelve years, he told Ila Mae—biding his time, waiting for the marriage to self-destruct and breathing our exhaust. He'd had time to plan our moral reform.

Pat must have been moved by his patience and his inarticulate longing. She filed for divorce, and within two weeks after Cy signed the papers, married the best man at her first wedding. No more living in a car or in the trailer, which vanished almost as soon as Roy unhitched it. We moved into a small house in Missoula, Montana, where Roy had a job with a wholesale candy and tobacco company and began to learn the ropes of what he called, grimly, "staying put, like sane people."

With his life savings, he took Pat shopping. In Lucy's Furniture Store, in an afternoon, they picked out a living-room suite, consisting of a beige sofa and matching armchair, both high on brass casters, both ponderous and both covered with the same kind of indestructible plush that is used to cover stuffed animals. They bought a Formica dinette set, slippery and cold to the touch, in mouse gray. They chose the china and silver plate that remained unused, thirty-seven years later, when Roy died.

It wasn't genteel to eat off the good china unless entertaining visiting heads of state. We used humbler dishes and graduated, in the fifties, to Melmac. Roy got us a plastic-handled set of knives, forks and spoons with Wrigley's bubble gum premiums.

For my room, they bought a bed, a bureau and a desk, at which I could apply myself to my schoolwork. I had a good mind, Roy told me, but like Cy, I was a grasshopper instead of an ant. With hard work, I could still aspire to ant status.

He put away our childish things, our boots and saddles. We saw no more of Pinky or my mother's other few remaining friends from the old days. We saw as little of Cy as the law allowed. While he was still my biological father, with visiting rights, this was a technicality. A father was the man who brought you up, not the handsome hell-raiser who breezed into town once in a while, on his way somewhere else, and left you "high-strung" for a week. Cy's very existence threatened Roy.

When Pat handed me over to him on the doorstep of the house, with Roy standing silently at her side, the old electricity between them hung in the air, heavy and palpable. They were still in love with each other, their divorce and Pat's second marriage another technicality. I had never heard of sex and I felt the tension between them. Roy felt it, and he had heard of sex.

There must have been hell to pay when the door closed, as there was when my mother got one of Cy's letters addressed to "Dear Cyra Sue and Pat." These, Roy tore open and shook out energetically to show us that no check for child support was enclosed. He also pointed out the obvious, that money doesn't grow on trees.

As a law student in North Dakota, Cy published his first piece of writing, a satire on the Charleston that begins:

> The Charleston is the name of a new form of physical exercise which is practiced on the ballroom floor, in fraternity and sorority houses, or in any place that a mental delinquent happens to become imbued with the desire to execute its intricacies for the amusement of those about him. This violent exercise, which is called a dance, differs from popular previous dance steps in that it requires more dexterity and less intelligence . . .

His prose style hadn't changed much when he began writing to Pat almost daily, ostensibly about my welfare. It was still flamboyant and stylish, full of posturing for her benefit but calculated not to offend Roy, the silent partner in their correspondence, who all but dusted those letters for fingerprints.

He also kept them all. Roy kept everything. Upstairs, in the succession of houses we rented, were the usual domestic trappings. The basements were archaeological sites, embedded with layer upon layer of letters, documents, old candy-order forms; age-whitened Life Savers and fancy boxes of petrified chocolates; every discarded item of clothing any of us ever owned; frayed inner tubes and snow shovels without handles, single surviving gloves of a pair, blankets turned into fine lace by moths. Roy was so compulsive a saver that when Pat threw something away, an old *Reader's Digest* or a soup can full of bacon grease, he went out to the garbage can in the alley, retrieved it and squirreled it away down in the basement.

Bacon grease, he believed, made roses grow to the size of cabbages, knowledge withheld from the general public by the fertilizer companies. We had no rosebushes, but we had our underground bunker full of bacon grease, and mice.

They ate the old chocolate, as well, but they didn't eat Cy's letters, probably because they were difficult to swallow. From Big Timber, where his return address was a friend's car dealership, he sent us a newspaper clipping from a Salt Lake City paper, showing a pretty eighteen-year-old with coyly downcast eyes nibbling on a pencil and contemplating her ballot for an election. "It was rather difficult to talk on the telephone to you the other night, as the young lady pictured on the enclosed was well within hearing distance." Hoping to be hired by one of Salt Lake City's radio stations, he continues, "I occupied myself with assisting at the mortuary." There he worked his magic on the mortuary owner's daughter. "I had informed her that I had no intention of again being married. Under these circumstances, she took enough phenobarbital, morphine and another kind of tablet to kill several persons."

A hardy creature, Miss Winifred L. pulled through, but not without leaving a hysterical suicide note addressed to Cy. "Under these circumstances, I thought it best to leave Salt Lake City."

In another letter, this one from California, he talks about enlisting in the Army so that he can choose his own branch of service instead of being drafted and says that if he's too old for the Aviation Corps, he'll join the Marines. "I would appreciate your reaction as Cyra's mother."

He mentions being delinquent in his child support, which he hopes to pay when he can sell the Packard, "a necessity that breaks my heart." He tells us about radio jobs promised and of rodeos for which he was almost hired before the "machinations" of some other announcer. He signs himself "Yours" and notes in a postscript, "Haven't had even a glass of beer in more than a *month!*"

Brilliantly manipulative, at once genuine and self-serving, these letters must have played chords on my mother's heartstrings. Into them, Cy tucks a picture of a lion cub, for me, and "a brochure with the finest explanation of Christ for a little youngster that I have ever seen. I happened to chance upon it at the mortuary."

Roy notwithstanding, he drops his guard now and then. Pleading to see me before he goes into the service, he tells Pat, "If I should become a casualty, several problems might be solved." I would inherit his service insurance. My mother would be freed of "our situation." All things considered, he might be worth more to both of us dead than alive.

How could Roy have competed with Cy's swagger and dash, or convinced himself that once he married Pat, the two of us would transfer our powerful affections? Though Cy would not agree to adoption, Roy changed my last name to his. He loved me, he told me, as if I were his own flesh and blood. He provided for me, according to his own ideas about what children need to prepare themselves for a world that rewards the deserving and punishes the slothful: brown oxfords instead of cowboy boots, a wholesome diet instead of hamburgers, indoctrination in the theory that whatever the task at hand, you attacked it with disproportionate zeal.

No chore was so routine, so trivial, that you could not compound it, washing the same window and polishing it with a chamois until the glass was so spotless you thought you were buffing thin air. Mowing the lawn in swatches that went up and down, back and forth, and then diagonally, though the grass cried out for mercy and could no longer be seen by the human eye. Sanding and varnishing the wooden panels of the family station wagon until you were hallucinating from inhaling varnish fumes. I still cannot wash a window without seeing Roy's red, sweating face on the other side and his finger tapping on the pane, pointing out an invisible smudge.

Work might not give you pleasure but it gave you dignity, which was better than bouquets thrown at your feet. Pat was a lost cause; her idea of hard labor was shaving her legs. My character, or lack of it, was not yet irreversibly determined; I could still be rescued. If only Cy wouldn't keep writing those letters, with plaintive requests that I write back in care of a bar in some cow town, and would stop turning up in Missoula, still nine feet tall to me in his boots and hat, the brim pinched jauntily into a Cheyenne roll. Stubbornly, I preferred boots to oxfords, rodeos to Lutheran vacation Bible camp, neither a camp nor a vacation.

Never one to shirk from duty, Roy found my re-education trying. The fly in the bacon grease was that I had "bad blood," my legacy from Cy.

His marriage to Pat, a consummation devoutly wished, was even more profound a disappointment. Briefly, she convinced herself that security was what she wanted most. She traded passion for it. She relinquished her footloose life, and Cy, for the plain, worshipful suitor who was his antithesis. Almost at once, she changed her mind, writing to Cy and receiving his letters through a post office box after Roy began opening all her mail. When she and I went grocery shopping, she phoned Cy from pay phones. In the back of her closet, she kept a suitcase packed and ready. Before a year was out, she grabbed it, and me, and got on a train. Cy had sent her the money to meet him in Denver, Colorado.

That last act of defiance determined the course of the rest of Pat's life. Whether she acted out of sheer wickedness, as Ila Mae said, or because conformity stifled her, or because of the pull of her feeling for Cy, she paid for it for forty years. The high-spirited colt no one could break, not even Cy, broke herself.

The compost heap that was our basement contained the history of that flight, which I knew little about because in Denver, my parents left me with relatives and took off for those few weeks by themselves. That Roy filed for divorce is on record; the document is intact, pain evident through the legal boilerplate. That Ila Mae got on the bus yet again and came to Missoula to be by Roy's side, I could have guessed. No one loved a melodrama more than she did, nor another piece of evidence that the world reserved suffering for those who least deserve it.

In the best of times, Ila Mae's letters are full of bankruptcies, house fires and illness beyond the reach of modern medicine. "The dr. says he's never seen anything like it, you wouldn't recognize him if you met him on the street, guess it's in God's hands now, he can't weigh more than seventy five pounds." Or: "Poor thing, well guess its for the best. She's out of this vail of tears now."

My aunt saw the world through morose-colored spectacles. If no one she knew was the victim of something sufficiently horrible, she included in her letters clippings from the newspaper: children abandoned by their mother, an old woman robbed on the street, a car wreck in which six people burned to death. Across the front of these enclosures, she scribbles, "Isn't this *terrible?*"

Solidly in Roy's corner, as Baby Sister burned down the barn again, she rose to new heights of outrage, bombarding my mother with two letters daily.

Dear Pat, just rec your card; Roy called me last nite I was so shocked that it has made me sick.

Ila Mae's health, it was a family conviction, was a fragile thing, her every breath drawn in torment. A lesser woman couldn't have borne it, much less kept on believing in God and putting up her own bread-and-butter pickles.

I am so disgusted with you to think you & Cy would try & pull something over on Roy . . . I have all ways stood by you when you left Cy for less. But this time I could beat your head off . . . You would have fit if you hadn't got your divorce from Cy so you could marry Roy Then to treat him this way: You aren't a child any more: I think you have back bone of jelly fish.

In the throes of emotion, my aunt always leaves out articles and punctuation.

Pat it isn't funny breaking a person heart and
some day you are going to find that out . . . If
you go back with Cy I will never visit if you
live with him 100 yrs for he doesn't like me
& I don't like him if I never see him again
will be too soon . . .

Her threat not to visit again might have been a
miscalculation, but she wound up with a zinger.
"Some day Pat your turn will come to reap what
you are sewing." There are a dozen of these letters,
all in what Ila Mae would have called the same
"vain," as well as more letters from Pat's other
sisters, mobilized from campaign headquarters in
Great Falls, and a letter from her old friend Pearl
in Billings.

This one scolds her at length and then suggests
she buy Ila Mae a fur coat: "They're so comforta-
ble for this cold country. It would last for years."
Ila Mae, Pearl adds as an afterthought, isn't well,
and furthermore, she's a grand sport.

Long-distance phone calls, in those days, were
still reserved for major life upheavals, too expensive for casual chat. When she phoned Pearl with
the news about Pat, my aunt must have thriftily
covered a second subject, the effect of Montana
winters on an invalid.

No fur coat materialized as a thank-you for
pointing out the path of righteousness. Cy was out
of work again, broke again and drinking again. He
and my mother must have made love again and
fought again, caught up in the patterns of provo-

cation and response that impose themselves upon a long marriage, grooves worn deep because they have been traveled so often.

Pat collected me and came home to Missoula, getting off the train, as she had when she left Arkansas all those years before, transformed. Her illusions were gone, and her fire. A soldier gone AWOL and now back in the trenches, she consigned herself to her second marriage.

Before their meeting in Denver, Cy had been a pariah in our new household. Now he became evil incarnate in boots. I was told not to mention his name.

He had joined the Army, Roy said. With luck, we'd never lay eyes on him again. I absorbed this information and had more spells, severe enough to warrant doctors, more needles and a health regime imposed by Roy.

The main feature was chewing every mouthful of food thirty times to "get the good out of it." Pat was also supposed to chew thirty times, to set a good example. Since we both cheated, Roy sat at the head of the dinette-set table, his eyes worried and watchful, and led us out loud in unison chewing. One, two, three, four . . . fourteen, fifteen, sixteen. The leaves changed color while we sat over a single dinner. Snow covered the ground. Spring came, and summer, followed by fall again. Or so it seemed to me, rhythmically revolving my jaw. Put cottage cheese on fork. Lift fork to mouth. Chew for eternity, while the earth rotates and your lifetime passes.

A health-food fanatic before health food was chic, Roy believed in the digestive tract the way some people believe in the one true path to the Buddha. Whole classes of food, everything I liked, would "repeat on you." French fries coated your stomach with grease, which never "passed"; it just sat there, turning you into a human grease trap. Not only should you eat an apple a day, you should eat the whole thing, core, seeds and stem. Briefly, before it proved unenforceable, Roy insisted that when ingesting oranges and bananas, you should eat the peel.

Harder to endure were his noon-hour tours around the Paxson Grade School playground in the station wagon, making sure I was wearing my snow pants. His method of curing head colds involved "sweating it out of you" with a portable heater and every blanket in the house. He doled out cod-liver oil by the shot glass. He believed in the healthy properties of fresh air.

Winter and summer, we left our bedroom windows open eight inches. At the end of my bed, October through February, would be a drift of new snow.

Worst of all was the mail-order house long underwear he made me wear, a peculiar peach color. Changing into gym bloomers in the school locker room was an exercise in humiliation, one more reason why I was miserable at school.

My speech was then an imitation of Cy's, inflated and full of big words, that made me seem a wizened, pretentious adult, whose only other con-

versational mode was swearing. Neither vocabulary
served me well as an icebreaker with either teachers or kids my own age.

I could already read, also considered eccentric,
but read from the last page to the first, the result
of long exposure to Burma Shave signs. Thank God
no one in Missoula then had heard of dyslexia.
Roy would have found a homegrown cure for it.

His anxiety about my health, I know now, orig-
inated in something real. If I romanticize Pat and
Cy's life together, their great love and greater talent for destructiveness, I can't romanticize the venereal disease my mother contracted before I was
born and for which she was being treated that last
summer in Billings. It ruined her own health and
made the family keep a worried eye on me.

Pat's post office box notwithstanding, Roy early
on managed to intercept her letters from Cy. The
parts of them he chose to read aloud, he read to
her. The paragraphs he chose not to read, he x'd
out, with thick, angry black lines. Some of these
letters explain Pat's mysterious illness.

"My report came back from the State Board of
Health yesterday and supplementing the report of
the local pathologist, it was entirely *negative*. Both
made Kahn tests in addition to Wassermanns so it
would seem quite conclusive that not even the
slightest possibility exists that I had ever been exposed." He goes on to beg her for the results of
the latest blood tests done on me. Guilt and worry
about us both, he says, have given him a great deal
of hell.

Venereal disease was considered so shameful then that Roy's and Ila Mae's anxious letters back and forth about Pat's condition used a code word for it: malaria. How her illness must have stigmatized my mother, tying a bell on her as a moral leper. How it must have strengthened Roy's hold over her, the authority of a stern parent over a child.

Only Cy sympathized, and refused to judge her, and Cy could no longer be part of her life. The Denver fling had driven that reality home. It also drove Pat home to Roy, prepared to lie in the bed she had made for herself.

SIX

~~~~~~

Plain men who marry beautiful women worry. With opportunity ever at hand, will they be betrayed? Jealous of Cy before the Denver episode, Roy had his answer. It filled him not just with anguish but with an increased sense of injured merit. "To my dear wife Pat," he had inscribed the picture of himself he gave my mother on their wedding day. "May all our days be as happy as this one." Now he tore the picture in half, in front of us both so that I would be aware of my mother's perfidy. Later he retrieved it from the garbage and saved it, as he saved his copy of the divorce complaint.

Paragraph II: "That ever since said marriage the plaintiff has been a good and faithful husband and has performed and discharged all of his marital duties and obligations, but that the defendant, totally disregarding the solemnity of her marriage vows, did voluntarily and wilfully commit adultery in that defendant engaged in sexual intercourse with one Cy Taillon."

For years it puzzled me that Roy so carefully preserved evidence of his humiliation. His pack-rat tendencies alone do not explain it. What does is that in the early years of their marriage he saw his claim to Pat, awarded him for years of single-minded devotion, as tenuous. She would leave him, if not with Cy, with some other man, and when she did, Roy would be left with something—pride-saving proof that he was the injured party.

None of us would be allowed to forget this, ever. If insufficiently impressed with my mother's appalling lack of rectitude, I might tap-dance to the same tune.

The torn and patched portrait, the divorce papers and the scolding letters from Ila Mae were also saved for me, hoarded against the day I would renounce Cy. Roy believed he was engaged in a tug-of-war for both Pat's soul and mine. He could not stop tugging long after Cy let go of his end of the rope.

Dear Cy,

I haven't answered your last letter because I've been doing a lot of thinking.

I realize now that you and I could never be together again with any kind of Harmony, too much water has passed under the bridge; but couldn't live with you for almost twelve yrs. without having a lot of memories, and our

having Cyra made those memories harder to
forget, but I am forgetting them and I know
its best for all concerned.

Written in pencil on lined paper, this letter is a
rough draft. Though it is signed "Pat," the hand-
writing is not my mother's but Roy's.

I like my home here with Roy and he has
been very good to both Cyra and I and the
fact that I am ——— ——— proves that he has
my interest and happiness at heart.

My guess is that Roy planned to dictate this letter to Pat, or stand over her while she copied it,
when he could think of the right words to fill in
the blanks. My mother now conducted all of her
affairs, without exception, through her second husband and life manager.

He made her weekly appointment at the beauty
parlor, drove her there, waited for her in the car
and drove her home. She gave him the grocery list
and he did the shopping, abolishing another pre-
text for her to leave the house and come within
dialing distance of a pay phone. When she went
bowling Tuesday nights, let out of her cell for an
exercise period, Roy and I went along with her.
Since Pat was allowed to bowl only on Ladies'
Night, an assignation at the alleys was unlikely.
Roy was taking no chances.

He enlisted me in these security precautions,

taking me aside and questioning me closely soon
after he got home from work. Had Pat talked to
any strange men while he was gone? Any man we
knew? Any men? If she'd talked to anyone on the
telephone, what had she said? He tried for casual-
ness while he conducted these interrogations, but
a smiling tormentor is still a tormentor. I remained
tight-lipped and wary even when he threw in the
promise of an ice-cream cone after dinner.

Half a dozen times a day, he phoned Pat from
work, making sure she was still nailed to the floor.
My mother took to leaving the bathroom door
open while she was on the toilet, offending my
sensibilities. I think she did this because it gave
her an extra second or two to hitch up her pedal
pushers and sprint for the insistently ringing telephone.

Sometimes she and I sat on the front porch on
hot afternoons, enjoying a Missoula pastime,
watching the lawn sprinklers. Neighboring housewives sat on their front porches too, visiting back
and forth and offering my mother the limited social exchange of "Hot enough for ya?" We never
had to wait long before the wood-paneled station
wagon slowly rounded the corner on patrol. Finding no strange car in the driveway, Roy sometimes
rolled down the window, waved and told us he was
"just passing by" on his delivery rounds.

Other days, he pulled his hat well down over his
eyes, looked neither left nor right and drove on.
Now almost totally bald, and self-conscious about

it, Roy never went out without a hat. Apparently he thought that if he pushed it down far enough, we couldn't see him.

Evenings we gathered around the radio. Roy lay on the sofa with his arms folded tightly across his chest and his eyes closed. Pat sat in the matching overstuffed chair, chain-smoking Lucky Strikes, and looked at some point in the middle distance. I lay on my stomach on the rug, doing homework.

We looked like a *Saturday Evening Post* cover, the family gathered round the Philco, listening to "The FBI in Peace and War," but this homey tableau was no more realistic than most. We talked not at all. Pat yawned now and then, out of boredom. Roy brooded, or slept, or pretended to sleep while he watched her through almost closed eyes. I tried to look busy over my arithmetic workbook while elaborating on my favorite fantasy: Cy coming to the door, with the Packard waiting at the curb, and taking me back to Billings, or Butte, or anywhere there were rodeos.

He needed me with him, he would explain to my mother and Roy, because he had so much work announcing he couldn't handle it all alone. I was a top hand at the mike and could work the crow's nest almost as well as he could, maybe better in a few years when I'd had more experience. So long, and we'd write from the road.

Next reel, me at the microphone, at a night rodeo, high above the arena. I'm spinning out long silk strings of words, like my father. I'm emanating the same star quality. I have new boots, since my old ones don't fit anymore. My hair flows down my back, beneath my white Stetson, and back in its element it is naturally curly. This gives me such a marked resemblance to Margaret O'Brien that everyone who sees me says I'm the spitting image. They're all amazed that they overlooked it before.

Caught up in this scenario, I went off to brush my teeth at eight o'clock dazed as a sleepwalker, and when I was in bed, left the door of my room open so that I could hear the doorbell. It never rang, except at the behest of a Jehovah's Witness or the Fuller Brush man, from whom Pat was afraid to accept the free sample in case Roy thought it evidence of intimacy.

After that first year of their marriage, my mother and Roy went nowhere as a couple and invited no one. A town the size of Missoula has few secrets. Pat's flight with Cy and Roy's cuckoldry had enlivened the party lines over a long, otherwise dull winter. They hadn't been a brilliant success in small-town society even before scandal made matters worse.

Social life in Missoula revolved around card parties, a few couples invited for bridge, highballs and small sandwiches, cut on the bias for elegance and filled with olive-pimento cheese spread. Pat went to these gatherings grudgingly. She hated bridge and played badly. Roy had once enjoyed them, but he did not enjoy being the object of curiosity and pity; and if they'd toughed it out and accepted invitations, they'd have had to reciprocate.

They had played host for their own card party

only once. The three of us spent a tense afternoon getting ready. Roy complained about Pat's sloppy housekeeping and her sandwich-cutting technique, pressing the bread down hard with outspread fingers and then sawing between them. The gluey white bread retained the imprint of her fingertips; each sandwich had craterlike squashed places in it.

Pat pursued the logic of the pecking order by yelling at me. In the interest of fairness, I had assigned myself the job of counting all the nuts in the paper nut cups to be sure that each guest got exactly the same number and nobody got more cashews than anyone else. Throughout these preparations, the air vibrated with our respective grievances and hurt feelings.

An hour into the soiree, Pat bungled a bridge hand. Roy addressed the guests on the subject of her shortcomings as card player and housewife, smiling an awful smile that included us all in the joke. My mother took these comments in the spirit in which they were intended, jumped to her feet and upended the card table into his lap.

Nut cups, scorepads, pencils, highballs, sandwiches and bridge mints scattered. So did the guests, thanking Pat and Roy for the lovely evening. The party lines must have hummed nonstop the next day.

Because friends' mothers did not throw tantrums and embarrass people, it hardened my heart against her that mine did. I was judgmental as only children are judgmental. I was desperate to conform to Missoula social norms. I was also too young to

know that all parents embarrass all children, if by
no overt act, by breathing.

The "good dishes," the green-stemmed wine and
water goblets Pat and Roy had picked out together,
the silver plate for twelve in its chest—gradually,
all were relegated to the backs of the kitchen cupboards, there to gather dust for thirty-five years.
The two of them gave no holiday open house with
Tom and Jerries served from the cut-glass punch
bowl. They invited no friends for supper, so they
never needed the mahogany-veneer drop-leaf table
in the living room. Roy put an ad in the newspaper
and sold these things. Bit by bit, he let go of his
own cherished fantasy, the backlit vision of domestic life with Pat he must have clung to
throughout all those lonely years in the boardinghouses.

In early snapshots of him is a Roy I never met.
He parts his already thinning hair in the middle,
slicks it down, smiles dashingly and puts an arm
around each of two pretty women in flapper dresses.
He poses in the bathtub of a boardinghouse, while
one friend scrubs his back with a long-handled
brush and another, playing the butler, offers him a
bottle of beer on a tray. He visits Yellowstone Park
with friends, in an open touring car, strikes pugilis-
tic poses in his boxing clothes and holds up strings
of trout he caught. He looks happy.

The yellowing old photos trace his transformation until he became the man my mother met,
prematurely middle-aged before he was thirty. He
doesn't smile anymore but stares at the camera with

a severe, humorless gaze. His body thickens and seems to take on gravity, a body not just heavier but somehow closer to the ground. What the photos don't tell me is what changed him, why he grew old and disappointed while still young.

All the adults I knew—neighbors, teachers, the man behind the grocery store counter—admired Old Honest Face. They told me how hard he worked and how good he had been to my mother and me. I should be grateful to him, they said, for treating me, a child not his own, as if I were his flesh and blood.

I endured these lectures shifting from one foot to the other, felt guilty for not being as grateful as people thought I ought to be and heard a faint undercurrent in all such tributes, the animosity people feel toward goodness that carries with it the whiff of self-congratulation. It won Roy admiration, but it didn't win him affection.

Cy, the reprobate, had hundreds of friends. Roy, virtue personified, had none, with the exception of Ila Mae, a kindred spirit. She visited us so often the intervals between visits seemed shorter than the visits themselves. Arriving on the Greyhound bus, for she and Wiley could not afford a car, she brought preserves, pickles and implacable good intentions.

She took over the kitchen and cooked all our meals, thereby, she suggested to Pat, staving off Roy's and my imminent starvation. She unearthed the chenille bedspreads we never used from the cedar chest, aired them on the clothesline and put them on the beds. "Now isn't that nicer, Patty?" She scrubbed the kitchen walls and woodwork with ammonia and water, bringing on one of her migraine headaches.

"You shouldn't have done it," Roy said. "Not with your health."

"Well, I had to, Roy," Ila Mae said in a small voice, from her bed of pain. She managed to imply that Pat's housekeeping was so bad we were about to be shut down for health code violations.

At dinner, she urged Roy to have third helpings. If there was one thing she loved, she said, it was to see a hungry man eat. Anyone who worked as hard as Roy deserved a good hot supper at the end of the day, and given her many other onerous responsibilities, who knew when she'd be back and he'd get another one?

Roy took her shopping for things she thought our household needed. They came home with a furry cover for the toilet seat, a flowered plastic cover for the toaster and one for the mixer. Ila Mae believed in covering things with other things: beds with bedspreads, chair arms with doilies, my mother with more clothes.

Pat's usual at-home costume was shorts or pedal pushers and a blouse with the bottom rolled up and knotted above her trim bare midriff. Ila Mae bullied her into the housedresses she ran up on her sewing machine, indestructible garments cut like flour sacks. Pat looked self-conscious and uncomfortable, like a dog children have dressed in doll clothes.

The way we were living, my aunt frequently announced, made her just sick. So did an endless list of other things—the inhumanity of man toward man, children who sassed, the absence of a butter knife on a butter plate—but in Pat's lackadaisical housekeeping she saw a chance both to do her Christian duty and to get her own back. No one had ever pelted Ila Mae with roses. It seemed unlikely that anyone ever would. She wasn't the Montgomery sister who'd been the "Toast of St. Louis" and she had few prospects of becoming the "Toast of Great Falls." Even her husband didn't appreciate her.

Gentle Wiley, once the most tractable of men, had learned to resist all attempts to improve his character by practicing passive resistance, paying no more attention to Ila Mae's nagging than to a dog barking somewhere way off in the distance. He spent his time at home barricaded behind his newspaper with a forbidden can of beer within easy reach. He no longer washed his hands on command.

Only Roy praised Ila Mae, admired her and held her up as an example to Pat. He fussed over her health. He gorged himself on her cooking ostentatiously, knife and fork flying to the accompaniment of blissful grunts, so that Pat didn't miss the point: Good Man Eating Good Meal Cooked by Good Woman. At the bus depot, when Ila Mae headed back to Great Falls, he told her that he couldn't thank her enough for everything she had done.

Ila Mae always said she only wished that she could have done more. She began to write to Roy in care of the candy company, private letters that stressed their mutual bond of sympathy. "Please Roy tear this letter up don't take it home," she begins one such missive, but she was appealing to the wrong man.

Ila Mae's letters in that period fill a good-sized box that once held overshoes. She wrote once a day and sometimes twice, in her usual breathless style and on any piece of paper that came to hand, including the backs of letters she had received herself. Waste not, want not. For material, she had Pat's infidelity with Cy to chew over, an event that could not be overanalyzed. She had her own frail health and Wiley's illness as well. In his mid-thirties, he'd had a stroke and was at death's door, she narrates, though his condition seems to exasperate more than worry her. She had her own romance with Roy's brother Vin.

Consummated or unconsummated, the product of her imagination or a real love affair—the details are missing, in the interest of discretion or because there weren't any—this passion flowered from one of her visits to us when Vin was visiting too.

Vin was a bachelor. Though he came to Montana looking for work, he spent his month or so with us lying on the sofa, drinking beer and snapping dish towels at Pat's rump, an entertainment that infuriated her but sent both Vin and Roy into fits of high-pitched whinnying. He was no charmer, in my opinion, since he had little use for children

other than as beer bringers, but Ila Mae found him
more attractive than I did.

It would seem hypocritical of her to chastise Pat
for a love affair and then indulge in one herself.
But my aunt's extramarital adventure, her letters
make clear, bears no resemblance to Pat's whatsoever, since Ila Mae's was divinely ordained. "Some
how I have a Feeling that God intended for Vin
& I to meet for God knows we couldn't help it."

Though written English fought her all the way,
she gave Cy stiff competition as a masterful manip-
ulator. Writing to Roy, tirelessly stirring up domestic unrest, she sought not just to conquer but
to divide.

Monday morning

Dear Roy:

Well how are things going better I hope. Roy,
Pat hurt my feelings when I got ready to leave
she never even as much said thanks all she
said was, she was glad that I came over, ask
Vin for he was there. But I know how you felt
about it: for as I told you that I will all ways
help you In any way That I can. any time.
You just let me know.

I know she was glad when I left.

The dinner at the restaurant was very nice
& She was nice as she could be . . .

"As nice as she could be" is a conventional
phrase. Ila Mae somehow gives it the subtext
"which we both know isn't very nice at all."

Wiley is in such condition I called the Dr. have appointment for 8 this evening he is going to have ex ray somehow I know that we will have to give up the House before Long & I just can't go back to his mother's to live. I will let you know how things turn out.

Finally comes the main business at hand:

. . . Pat has written to Hope about Cy calling all the time & Hope is such cat that she has spread it all over town. I told Pat long ago that you can't trust her. Please Roy don't tell her any thing I tell you because I know you are right & will all ways do the right thing.

"Cy calling all the time . . ." The words must have detonated within Roy like a bomb. He could intercept letters and destroy them. Must he also have the phone ripped out? Surround our bungalow with a moat? Hire a team of sharpshooters trained to fire at anybody wearing a cowboy hat? Leaving him reeling in the shock waves, Ila Mae winds up briskly.

. . . Will let you know how Wiley comes out he looks half dead.

Busy though she was fanning all those flames, Ila Mae did not neglect my mother's moral guidance or mine. To Pat, she wrote: "Pat dear you have such lovely home & the grandest husband I

pray to God to help you & keep you good sweet
& loyal all ways." And to me: "Hello Susie have
you been good little girl. Remember when you are
naughty that God puts a mark on the Board."

She closes with the promise that she is going to
send me "nice Bible book." I doubt that I so much
as looked at the pictures. To my well-intentioned
aunt, I owe my continuing resistance to all forms
of religious belief. Though her own faith was genuine, and though she believed that godliness was
next to cleanliness, she instilled in me the conviction that God, like Ila Mae and Roy, was a keeper
of old scores, the type cowboys would say had Himself a burr under His saddle.

SEVEN

Wiley recovered and went back to selling men's clothing at Strain Bros. department store, where he got a little respect as "our Mr. Gosney." Vin went back to Wisconsin, without Ila Mae. She wrote Roy that she would not have gone with him even if he'd asked. My mother and stepfather went on with the accommodation that would become a long marriage. Inscrutable, I once considered it, but I am now older and I do not think of marriages as scrutable.

Theirs made as much sense as any. Pat was childish herself, incompetent at the practical business of living and saddled with a young child. She needed refuge and may have thought of it as temporary, from one day to the next, until the days added up to years and she no longer thought of it at all. Roy was used to disappointment: the gold strike, when he was a miner, that somehow made someone else rich, the innocent schemes for self-improvement he pursued—business school correspondence courses, health food and miracle vitamins, potions and unguents for growing hair—that led nowhere and left him unchanged. His marriage to my mother was just one more.

Roy never gave up trying to reverse his baldness. It pains me still that I once humiliated him by giving him a pair of military brushes for Christmas. He opened the package, then left the room, choking out that I'd done it now and this time I was going to catch it. Pat laughed helplessly. I wondered what I had done and why he did not like my gift. It wouldn't help matters now if I could explain to Roy that I didn't see him as bald because I didn't see him at all.

While I had not seen Cy for months either, he still held me in the same thralldom and his distant star eclipsed Roy. The parent on the scene making the rules cannot compete for glamour with the one who is not there, and when the rules include chewing each mouthful of food thirty times, there is no contest.

Nor could Roy compete with Cy in knowing how to charm me, though he longed for my affection and tried hard to win it. He gave me a watch for my birthday, a gift he could ill afford. Cy sent a telegram, delivered to our front door by messenger, and dazzled me; I knew of no other child who had ever received a telegram. "Isn't that just *typical*," said Ila Mae, who was there. "Scaring us all like that. I thought sure it was from Wiley, and his mother had passed away."

For Christmas, Roy gave me the bicycle I'd

longed for, secondhand but lovingly repainted, and had to watch while I exclaimed over it briefly, set it aside and went back to pawing over Cy's gift, a package full of smaller packages. Individually wrapped, these contained every food I loved and was no longer allowed to eat: a tall jar of stuffed green olives, the kind I used to fish out of my parents' martinis; animal crackers; Kraft's caramels; marshmallows; Tootsie Rolls; a dozen Hershey bars. Roy's face told me that before I had taken a bite out of these, he could hear my teeth starting to rot.

Cy's letters came, addressed to me. A man was entitled to write to his daughter, if not to his ex-wife, so Roy reluctantly let the mail go through. Though I could read them perfectly well myself, Pat helpfully volunteered to read these letters to me and was less puzzled than I was, I'm sure, by such information as: "In the event you are interested, I haven't had a date in the last two and a half months. I tried keeping company with a girl in Salt Lake City but despite the fact that I am continually lonesome as Hell for someone ... I haven't been able to make a go of it and despite myself have been drawn into a shell from which it is difficult to emerge."

He was bouncing around the country again, finding little work and hard up. From Tucson, and Phoenix, and a dozen other western towns, he wrote letters, ostensibly to me, about prospects and reversals. "Next week, M-G-M begins the filming of *Apache Trails* here and I hope to obtain work on that until my shows get under way." "I was offered a show at St. Louis for March 25–April 1st but I guess my price was too high as I have not heard from them." "It will be necessary for me to dispose of the car in some manner which I hope to determine within the next few days. There remains a balance of $272.20 and I do dislike to lose an investment of $1300.00 because of that amount. Yet . . . I have to have some cash to go on until February unless something breaks in the meantime."

He didn't get the job as a movie extra. He didn't get the radio announcing job he wanted at a small station in Harrisonburg, Virginia. He left a job as a ranch hand because "the situation there became practically unbearable" and holed up on another ranch owned by a friend, to "get out the scores of letters incident to lining up my itinerary for this, my final year in this game."

Desperate, he finally sold the Packard, in Salt Lake City, for a few hundred dollars. It broke his heart, he wrote, and it also broke Pat's. Reading this news to me, she cried.

The midnight-blue Packard had been our announcement to the world, and ourselves, that we Taillons were winners. It had style, that ephemeral thing Pat and Cy valued above all else. It represented the old, footloose high-roller days, and no sensible Plymouth station wagon, its fenders and hood a muddy maroon, could inspire the same pride of ownership. That Cy would part with it was unthinkable.

Roy, Pat and I all knew that Cy could not have brought himself to sell the car unless he was flat broke. Only Roy found that knowledge heartening. Though Cy enclosed a crisp fifty-dollar bill, in partial payment of overdue child support, the money was not as welcome as the news that "the Big Shot," as Roy called Cy, was in a tailspin and rapidly losing altitude.

My parents' divorce agreement, unusual at the time, provided that each had custody of me for six months of the year. Pat was to take me for the school year, Cy for the summers and school vacations.

My spending school vacations with him was impractical, since he was usually thousands of miles away. Summers were also out of the question. He was working rodeos then, and in Roy's and Ila Mae's views, couldn't take care of me properly. Still spindly and neurasthenic, I could not survive three months of hard travel, hamburgers and Hershey bars. So I saw Cy only when he came through Missoula. Because these visits were infrequent, and because Cy staged each like a Broadway play, they became big events not just for me but for Missoula, anticipated with as much interest as the opening day of deer-hunting season.

Missoula is a pretty town with numerous virtues. Spectacle and diversion are not among them, unless one counts watching car crashes at an intersection called "Suicide Junction." Cy's appearances were at least as exciting, and nobody died.

Forbidden by Roy to come to our house anymore, he picked me up at Paxson Grade School. I knew he was in the building before I actually saw him because he stopped in at the principal's office to find out which classroom I was in. Through the office secretary, or a miscreant kid putting in detention time, word leaked out the door that some cowboy movie star was in our midst.

Next came the sound of Cy's boot heels down the hall, accompanied by pairs of other feet. In the course of his progress from the first floor to the second, he'd picked up a retinue. Trotting behind him were the principal, female teachers and kids who were supposed to be somewhere else. All that was missing was a marching band playing "I Love a Parade."

I'd hear his unmistakable baritone, pitched for the bleachers, telling how he'd always wanted to teach school himself, because there was no job like it. Oh, not for the material rewards, maybe, but for the satisfaction.

Finally he stood in my classroom door, handsome as Gary Cooper, in his whitest hat and nattiest Western shirt and narrow-legged pants, with his beautifully manicured hands resting on an enormous silver and gold belt buckle. "Cy Taillon," he introduced himself, lifting his hat to my teacher, who looked breathless. On one of these occasions, he got a spontaneous round of applause from the third grade.

Manic with joy at seeing him again, I was anxious to leave school and have him to myself, but

not Cy, surrounded with admirers. He let himself
be persuaded to give an informal talk about rodeo,
the only all-American sport, while the principal
beamed and took a seat and thought this was his
own idea. "I guess you've heard about enough,"
Cy said, at intervals. "No, no," screamed his rapt
audience.

He'd seen what looked like a fine instrument
through the open door of the music room, Cy mentioned. He played a little piano himself. Soon he
was installed on the bench putting the old upright
through his rendition of "Springtime in the Rock-
ies," heavy on trills suggesting birdsong. He captured everyone within range of his voice, roughly
the southwest quadrant of Missoula, with stories of
his travels across America, the grandest country in
the world. He had us all, kids and adults, jumping
through hoops.

Cy was not being paid for this performance, but
things were slow on the circuit and an audience
was an audience. He would have gladly done two
shows, called a square dance and then pitched War
Bonds in front of the PTA. Appreciation was the
little bottle labeled "Drink Me" whose elixir made
him tall, taller, taller still.

By the time I finally got him out of there, by
threatening to have hysterics, he had a date with
the red-haired music teacher to discuss my buried
talent for music (still buried so deep it has never
surfaced); an ink stain on his middle finger from
signing autographs with a school pen; a satisfied
flush under his suntan. The music teacher believed

Cy had always wanted to be a concert pianist—if only he could have had lessons, instead of being entirely self-taught. The principal knew Cy thought being principal of Paxson Grade School the noblest of callings. The girls in the class all wanted to grow up to be Miss Rodeo America, and the boys champion bronc riders.

Was everybody happy? Everybody except my father, who deflated visibly when we were by ourselves and the performance was over. Demonstrating that he was not bound by Roy's relayed injunctions, he took me out for greasy food. He told me how much he'd missed me and read the report cards I'd saved up for him. But he was restless, gazing out the car windows as we sat in the drive-in parking lot, not even bothering to flirt with the car hop.

He asked me about my mother. How was her health? Did she have headaches anymore? How was she wearing her hair now? Did she still sing that damned song all the time around the house? He meant "Stormy Weather," Pat's staple along with "Rain or Shine." She was fond of songs about love under assorted climatic conditions.

Before he dropped me the block from home Roy permitted, Cy gave me a letter for her, with instructions to deliver it when Roy was not around. It was nothing to do with Roy, he said, just news about old friends.

I gave him the letter Pat had tucked into my lunchbox, uneasy because I was sure that Roy would not approve and that he would find out. He missed nothing, my stepfather, no invisible speck on a freshly washed window, no blade of grass left standing on a lawn mowed so closely it looked as if it had been cropped by sheep, no subversive act of Pat's or mine, real or suspected.

Sometimes I stared at him absentmindedly. "I know what you're thinking," Roy was inclined to announce on such occasions. Whatever it was, he didn't like it and repaid my stare with odd forms of reprisal. Most unbearable was no reading other than school books, enforced by night raids to make sure I wasn't reading by flashlight under the covers. Second most unbearable was helping clean out the garage, a useless undertaking consisting of shifting piles of things, the overflow from the basement, from one damp, spider-infested corner to the other. As a middle-aged adult, I have yet to live in a house with either a garage or a basement.

What form Pat's punishments took, I don't know, since house arrest does not permit many embellishments. Whatever the risk, she continued to stay in touch with Cy by whatever means she could contrive.

In 1942, a few months before he enlisted in the Army Air Corps, Cy wrote Pat a three-page typewritten letter advising her to have an abortion. Her own letter to him, appealing to him for advice, had followed him around for weeks, from temporary address to temporary address. It filled him with confusion, coming "as a considerable additional shock to those of the past few years." He had no right to enter into any decision she might make, he wrote, but he was full of concern for her state of mind—"It is the grossest kind of an injustice to bring an unwanted child into the world"— and her health. "You are still taking treatments and if you intensify these again as you did before, there is a great possibility that your health will be impaired to a great extent. Moreover, in consideration of the fact that this condition of yours continues to persist, you will be taking a tremendous chance for the baby. Do you think it would be fair to subject an unborn one to the chance?"

They were lucky with me, he says, in that my periodic tests do not indicate any disease. Pat cannot count on being as lucky a second time.

His usual eloquence trails off into near-incoherence: "Regardless of what our actual feelings toward each other may be—or, regardless of what may develop in the future—if you do feel as you have indicated, and, in consideration of all that you are going through now . . ."

Beginning "Dearest Pat" and ending "All my love," this is my father's valedictory letter to my mother. It hints at their continuing longing for one another while acknowledging that he has no further claim on her. "In the light of your quickly chosen circumstances, I really have no right to make any further suggestions regarding you or your relationship to me." It tells her that "the thoughts that your letter aroused in my mind are far too involved to write." Write him as soon as possible with regard to her decision, Cy pleads; he will always be of any help he can be to her. But he was letting go of her at last. Whether she had the baby or not, Pat was pregnant by Roy. There could be no more tangible proof that she was his wife now.

No baby was born. My mother's medical condition may have made it possible for her to have a legal abortion, or she may have made the private arrangements women then and now contrive to make if they are desperate enough. I don't know, either, whether she ever received Cy's letter or whether Roy intercepted and withheld it. All I do know about her pregnancy is that Ila Mae was never consulted. Had she been, another boot-box would have bulged with her counsel on the subject, along with privileged information on what God thought about it.

Later that year, Pat had a nervous breakdown. I was told she was visiting Ila Mae. She was actually in a sanitarium called Warm Springs. A ceaseless flow of letters from Ila Mae harangued Roy about feeding me properly and seeing that I went to Sunday school, discussed Pat's "malaria" as the cause of her emotional problems and blamed Cy for her physical and moral deterioration. "Before she met him she was sweetest thing ever lived." Ila Mae hadn't thought so at the time but she wasn't a slave to foolish consistency.

Roy should "keep chin up," she told him, and enclosed a note for Pat telling her to think of Roy and do everything the doctors ordered, "for they know what's best for you."

My mother's sister Lucille also wrote to her, from the Wisconsin dairy farm where she lived with her

second husband. Her first had been a Filipino railroad engineer named Pedro Magatutu, a union that
must have raised eyebrows back home in Paragould. Pedro was seduced by the music of the rails,
and vanished. Lucille settled down with Henry and
the dairy herd. "You make Roy happy and *forget*
the past,"she wrote Pat. "I know about the hap-
hazard life you've led, & dear was it worth it? I'm
lots older than you and I want you to be happy
with Roy as I am with Pa. It takes a man with a
little more age & yes common sense to make a
woman appreciate her good fortune."

Did Pat hear, in her sisters' words of comfort,
their mutual belief that she was being punished for
her sins? Her therapy involved drugs, spinal taps
and something called "brain waves"; she must
have been ready to believe it.

Once in the two months she was gone, she
phoned, reassuring me that she was all right, only
having such a swell time with Ila Mae that she was
staying longer. She also told me to be good, one
of those parental injunctions she rarely uttered.
She'd been on the receiving end of it too often.

No uncritical expression of love and sympathy
came from Cy this time, for no one told him about
Pat's breakdown, though Lucille's letter mentions
that she and Pa have heard from him. "Cy writes
us he may join the Army, just where he belongs."
The family's consensus was that he was in no way
involved, other than as a guilty bystander.

While my mother was gone, Roy and I made a
qualified peace with each other. He lectured and

scolded me less. I tried harder to please him, aware
that something I did not understand was causing
him pain and worry. In return for my grudging efforts at housekeeping, he granted me an allowance
for the first time, a quarter a week. All his life,
Roy carried a change purse, an old-fashioned black
leather pouch with a clasp that opened with a snap.
Doling out my allowance, he opened it slowly and
deliberately, shook it to inspect its contents and
then handed over the two dimes and a nickel with
care, as if the coins were breakable.

What money Roy earned, he earned for six-day
weeks of hard work, and though he managed to
put a little aside, he never had more than he
needed. The trouble he had parting with it was
commensurate with the trouble he had getting hold
of it in the first place.

It puzzled me, his insistence that even a penny
was precious, worth stooping to pick up from the
sidewalk. It angered Roy that he could not get it
through my head that money was not manufac-
tured inside slot machines and that before it ended
up carelessly scattered up and down a bar, the shiny
silver dollars and the crumpled bills, someone had
to earn it. I thought money fell out of the sky, he
said, like Cy, and would end up the same way,
broke and a bum, unless my quarters went into the
bank he gave me and stayed there.

They went in, but they came out as fast. I had
learned to work the coins out through the slot on
top, armed with determination and a table knife I
kept hidden underneath my mattress. An adult

lifetime later, I still feel guilty when I spend money and guilty when I save it, caught between two powerful object lessons.

What money buys, Roy taught me, is security. What it ought to buy, Cy taught me by example, is self-respect, that fragile intricate form of it that people understand only when they have no security whatsoever. The ethic of the rodeo circuit was that if you won prize money for an event, you paid some less fortunate cowboy's entry fees in the next event. You also saw to it that he could hold his head up in the bar after the rodeo, which meant not buying a drink but buying a round and leaving the bartender the change. The money was a loan, but a loan that would never be called in.

The ethic around our household in Missoula was that self-respect came only at the price of honest labor. A handout, however well meant, degraded the receiver. In those post-Depression years of the early forties, tramps appeared at our screen door sometimes, asking to cut firewood, or mow the lawn, in exchange for a meal or a dollar. They terrified Pat, but Roy had forbidden her to turn them away, no matter how shabby they were.

Tell them to come back in the evening, he made her promise. If they did, he found some job for them and showed them where we kept our tools in the garage. He never stood over their shoulders while they did some task that did not really need doing, or conducted an inventory of the tools before they left. When the man came to the back door again, Roy met him with change purse in hand. "Here's your wages," he said gravely, and shook hands.

My father and my stepfather both understood dignity. They only understood it differently, a matter of temperament. Both were midwestern farm boys who left home and came out West, where there was room for ambition. Both fell in love with Pat, whose attraction for them must have been that she embodied no trace of girl-next-door, unless you happened to live next door to a burlesque house. They were more alike than they knew, and had my mother not come along, they might have remained friends until they were old men, Roy riding the tail of the comet, Cy grateful for the ballast.

EIGHT

As good as his word, Cy enlisted in the Army Air Corps. Friends had urged him to somehow remarry my mother in order to avoid the draft, he wrote to me, but he was outraged "at the apparent fact that someone would think that I would use the subterfuge of hiding behind the skirts of any woman to escape an obvious duty." "Subterfuge" sent me to the dictionary at school, to look up the word. Cy's letters frequently sent me burrowing through the dictionary, educational fallout from his letter-writing style.

He was ready to dispute with anyone "that I should fall into the category of being a coward," a thought that would have occurred to no one, not even Roy, who'd ever seen my bantamweight father pile into a fight. I was proud of him and terrified. From the way Roy and Ila Mae talked about Cy's joining the Army, I had the strong impression that he'd get killed, at least if he had

enough decency left in him to do the right thing
for once.

The months before he was assigned to duty were
the worst months of his professional life thus far.
Rodeo job after rodeo job fell through because of
cancellations. The country had other things on its
mind, and without the Packard, Cy had to travel
between the few announcing jobs he scraped up
on crowded wartime trains. While this was expensive, he wrote, it was still cheaper than trying to
run a car in the face of gas and rubber shortages.

To keep body and soul alive, he went back to
Salt Lake City in the hope of getting a job at the
Remington plant there, but he could not hold out
for the two or three weeks it took to get hired and
so signed on as a track laborer at an ordnance
plant, for sixty-five cents an hour. He said the job
saved him money on manicures.

What money he did not need to live on, and he
was living cheaply, he'd send on to Pat to buy
school clothes for me. Though Roy kept pointing
out that Cy was a deadbeat who owed him hundreds of dollars in child support, he took his obligation seriously at that point, and when he
could not send cash—always the crisp new bills he
liked to carry instead of worn ones—he at least
worried about it. Again he mentioned the $10,000
in service life insurance he was assigning to me.
He too seemed to think it likely I would collect.
The drifty, demoralized summer behind him had
left him pessimistic about his prospects in general.

An old shoulder injury, the result of his last attempt at bronc riding, kept Cy out of combat. As
he'd feared, he was too old to be a pilot, a major
disappointment. For all his posing and posturing,
his idea of serving his country involved more than
the public relations slot he soon found himself in.
He sent clippings of himself, dapper in uniform,
leading dance bands and acting as m.c. for bond
drive evenings and air shows. As usual, he underlined his name, frequently misspelled, in case I
managed to miss it while reading the photo cap-
tions. Letter after letter, he fumed about being on
the sidelines of the war and vowed not to give up
on being assigned to combat duty. Having failed
other tests of manhood, in others' eyes and his
own, he longed for another, one he knew he would
pass.

Then his letters stopped coming, an unprecedented and alarming lapse. Though my own letters
were less frequent than Cy's, though I saw him
briefly and seldom and though I was settling into
my new life with my mother and Roy, I basked in
the certainty of my father's love. He sent me birthday telegrams and Christmas boxes full of things
that were associated, in my mind, with the old
days. He still addressed me as Taillon instead of
Qualley, though Pat instructed me to write him
that she could call me anything she wanted. He
wrote me every two weeks, even when I didn't
write back or wrote the letters children write when
they are rebelling against an emotional claim: Dear
Dad, How are you? I am fine. I got a B in spelling.

P.S. My mother says to tell you she needs the money and send it.

Never had he stopped writing, no matter where he was or what was happening to him. As the months went by, I began to believe that he had been killed.

Even in peaceful Missoula, reminders that there was a war on were constant. At school, we took up collections to buy War Bonds. At home, Roy started a Victory garden, digging up our backyard and planting carrots, potatoes and onions, "good keepers" in case our food supply was cut off. A skillful farmer, he grew so many vegetables that we could supply our neighbors and still have enough to stockpile in a dank corner of the basement, smelling of earth and filling me with horror. I saw a lifetime ahead of eating cooked carrots.

Like everyone else, we saved flattened tin cans, cooking fat and string. When kids asked why the soldiers needed cooking fat and string to fight the Germans, no convincing answers were forthcoming. Adults didn't seem to know either. It was all part of "the war effort." We got the impression that they considered the question smart-alecky if not treasonous.

Ours not to question why. Ours to compete over who could make the biggest string ball and thank our lucky stars we weren't the children of Europe, who were being bombed and starving. When the March of Time newsreel at the Wilma Theater showed air raids, the cylindrical bombs dropping from the bellies of the planes, a girl I knew, at the movies with her parents, screamed that we were all going to be killed, a possibility that visited itself upon me as her parents led her, sobbing, up the aisle.

I caught her fear. The sight of a plane in the clear skies over Missoula turned me weak-kneed and made me lose bladder control. In bed, I heard the snarling engines in the newsreels again and waited for the explosion that would blow us all to smithereens.

Don't be ridiculous, Pat and Roy said, standing in the doorway of my room when nightmares made me cry out. Nobody was going to bomb South Central Avenue. The war was a long way away. We were winning it.

Kids who'd lost their older brothers came to school silent and swollen-eyed and suffered the awkward, unctuous sympathy of the rest of us. The newspaper announced additions to the list of "Gold Star Mothers." Evenings, the kids on my block were shooed out into our front yards while our parents listened to the news on the radio. When we were called in again, to sit down to supper, they were in no mood to tolerate complaints about the ration-coupon fare.

The adults knew more than they were telling us, it was clear, and maybe what they knew was that we weren't winning at all. We were losing. Still no letters from Cy; I knew he'd been sent into active combat, as he longed to be, someplace where the bombs were falling.

"You do what your father tells you," Pat said to

me over the dinner table one night, backing Roy up on some point of contention between us, such as the palatability of turnips. "My father's dead," I said, and burst into noisy sobs that were both self-dramatizing and born of real fear. Only the vehemence with which Pat denied it convinced me otherwise. My outburst caused the blood to drain out of her face and make her hands shake, so that she couldn't steady the match to light her cigarette.

Roy pushed back his chair and left the kitchen table. I bolted from it too, and in my room went back to work rolling string, superior heavy cord that Roy brought home for me from the candy company. It came on packing crates, he said, and if I kept up the good work, rolling it nice and tight like that, I might get a prize from the War Department.

I had the awards ceremony planned out in my mind, complete with a band and a famous general presenting me with the plaque. It pleased me to think how the people who found me an oddity, too fond by half of ten-dollar words, would have to revise their opinions and apologize or not get a seat in the auditorium.

When I'd last heard from my father, he'd been stationed in New Jersey. I wrote him a long, patriotic letter that would reach him somehow, I thought, if he were on some secret mission but still alive. I wrote him again, and again, and when I could find nothing to write, sent him newspaper clippings, content irrelevant; the point was an excuse to ask Pat for a stamp. I changed my tune and wrote dramatic letters berating him for not writing to me anymore, his very own daughter, the best string saver in Missoula. No answer over the weeks. I wrote him that I had a fatal disease and was dying. Weak as I was, and despite how hard it was to hold a pencil, I wanted to say goodbye.

Though Cy knew this was hokum, concern about my health must have been at the back of his mind constantly. He called Pat, late at night after I was in bed. She told him I was just fine, and what was it to him? He told her that he was getting married again. He must have stopped writing because he was afraid to break this news, not to me, but to her.

Pat's replay of this conversation to me was flat and don't-give-a-damn. She couldn't remember the woman's name, she said, and offered no information except that she was twenty-eight. An old maid.

My reaction was outrage that Cy hadn't consulted me. I made up a form to send him regarding my future stepmother: name, date of birth, height, weight, hair color, color of eyes, hobbies, favorite movie star, health (good? average? excellent?) but I lost my nerve before I mailed it.

They were already married by the time I met Dorothy, the girl who had seen Cy playing one of the twin pianos in the window of a Great Falls music store, when she was fourteen, and told a girlfriend, "Someday I'm going to marry him." The story was one newspapers loved and reprinted for thirty years.

An Army nurse, Dorothy had masses of auburn hair, a voluptuous body supported on short, thick legs, and enormous green eyes, extraordinary eyes that seemed to fill up her entire face. They glistened as if with tears all the time and gave her a wistful expression even when she smiled. She emphasized them with emerald-green eye shadow and a heavy black line on each upper lid.

Her hair was shoulder-length and artfully curled. She wore stylish, fitted gabardine suits, never slacks, and high-heeled backless pumps, called "Spring-o-lators," always color-matched to the rest of her clothes, heavy pancake makeup and jewel-toned pillbox hats. Her earrings matched everything else, her perfume preceded her into a room, and young as she was, she had adopted a notion of elegant style, furred, hatted and gloved, suited to a much older woman. One thing you could say for her, she said of herself, was that she knew how to dress.

I'd never seen anyone as glamorous as Dorothy and was stunned. She must have been taken aback by Cy's rail-thin, somber daughter, dark-skinned, pigtails pulled so tight they made my own eyes look slanted. Having prepared for our meeting by reading etiquette books in the Missoula library, I greeted her with "It's a pleasure to make your acquaintance."

This did not get our relationship off to the smooth

start I had intended, but nothing I could have said or done would have improved matters much. For Dorothy, I was evidence that my mother existed; that she had been Cy's wife for twelve years; that while Cy could sever every other tie, he had a child by a former show girl whose own beauty and style had made her a celebrity in Dorothy's hometown. I was the hard fact that interfered with the mythmaking of perfect love, burning uninterrupted with a true flame since the piano player and the schoolgirl locked eyes through the music store window.

The two of them were staying at Dorothy's parents' house in Great Falls, home on leave, when I went to visit, riding the bus as I'd always ridden the bus to catch up with Cy somewhere or other. The Cosgriff family, Dorothy's parents and a sister living at home, took me in warmly. They were a close, devoutly Catholic bunch, one with whom Cy must have felt at home, and they seemed to have enough of everything to go around and extend to me, rooms, beds, delicious food and tolerant good humor. If they also found me exotic, a gnome inclined to oratorical flourishes, they were kind about it. They were getting used to Cy's oratorical flourishes and willing to get used to mine.

Dorothy took my hair out of the pigtails and rolled it up on metal curlers. Like all previous efforts to curl my hair, hers failed. The reason, she told Cy and the rest of the family, was that I had impossible hair, as straight and fine as a cat's. She let me rummage around in her jewelry box and gave me a pair of earrings she no longer wore be-

cause they matched a dress she no longer had. I
had no use for earrings but knew she meant the
present as a goodwill gesture and was so effusive in
my thanks I must have unnerved her again. Letting
me try on one of her uniforms, she pointed out
that her own waist was so small it almost fit. My
mother had a really tiny waist too, I said, and got
a look from Cy that created a wind-chill factor in
the warm room. When he and I sat side by side on
the sofa later that same night, Dorothy came into
the room, ignored a pair of empty armchairs and
wedged herself between us.

"Dorothy, for god's sake," Cy said, at once
amused and irritated. I moved over so that the
three of us were not squeezed together but felt like
an inadvertent troublemaker again.

I went back home to Missoula a day later, and
with some childish impulse to wound, regaled Pat
with praise of Dorothy, her auburn hair, her green
eye shadow, her diamond engagement and wedding rings and her Spring-o-lators. I told her about
the photo I'd seen of her in her nurse's uniform,
carrying the American flag at the head of a parade.
To my disappointment, Pat asked no questions at
all, nor showed any interest in this monologue.
Only when I produced the plastic button earrings
Dorothy gave me did she betray curiosity. She took
the earrings over to the kitchen window and turned
them over in her hands, examining them as if they
were jigsaw pieces.

Whether by remarrying, or drying out, or both,
Cy had redeemed himself in Ila Mae's eyes. She

had seen him and Dorothy when they were in
Great Falls, my aunt wrote to my mother, and "Pat
you wouldn't recognize him he different man,
handsome as dog." The drying out was Dorothy's
doing. "He hasn't had single drink for mos. She
said it was either the bottle or her take his choice.
They don't any of them touch a drop, any of her
people." This was a miracle and proof of God's
grace, as Ila Mae had told Cy to his face. As for
Dorothy, she had to give her credit. Before she
came along, he was headed "straight for gutter."

I was sixteen or so when Dorothy gave me her
own account of Cy's reform. She had not only
made him swear that he would never take another
drink, but on their wedding night had insisted that
he get down on his knees and pray to God, for
help in keeping his word, before he climbed into
bed. She and I were in a motel room in Puyallup,
Washington, waiting for Cy to come back after
announcing a night rodeo. When he appeared, I
could not look him in the eye and snapped on the
television set.

The scene stays in my mind still, hilarious and
disturbing as a Thurber cartoon. In it, Cy kneels
beside the bridal bed in his boxer shorts and his
cowboy boots.

Some women believe that the right woman, loving and resolute enough, can dry out a drunk and
turn a lady-killer into a happily monogamous husband. In my view, this is like believing you can
win at three-card monte. Yet with Cy and Dorothy, I saw it happen. My father became a man I

barely knew, a new Cy impeccable in his starched uniform, clear-eyed and confident, within months after their marriage.

He walked differently. His old swagger had given way to a brisk, military step compromised somewhat by his bowed legs but impressive anyway. His manners with Dorothy were courtly; he opened car doors for her and held her coat, each of these acts ceremonious. To me, he observed that ladies did not sit with one ankle perched on the other knee and that there were also places well-brought-up little girls did not scratch. When I swore in his presence, he threatened to wash my mouth out with soap. Shades of Roy and Ila Mae. I was amazed.

Through laser looks and a stiffening of his body, as he sat behind the wheel of a car or on the sofa in Dorothy's parents' living room, he let me know that our old lives were now off-limits in conversation. "Remember . . ." I would begin, or "We used to . . ." and there would emanate from Cy what felt like a blast of cold air, freezing out both reminiscence and me.

The same cold draft chilled us all when Cy addressed me as "Pat," a mistake he corrected in the same breath but that left him flustered and Dorothy annoyed each time it happened. How much or how little Dorothy knew about Cy's first marriage, the powerful attachment, the destructive behavior and the refusal to acknowledge that it was over, she knew enough to feel threatened. If mentioning Pat was unavoidable, my mother was "her." "You'd better call Missoula and let her know when

Cyra's coming home." The pronoun came out of my stepmother's mouth with backspin on it. Without having it spelled out for me, on my short and infrequent visits, I knew that Dorothy felt the sooner I was back on the bus, the better.

Soon after the marriage she resigned her commission, while Cy, unwilling to be outranked by his wife, went into Officer Candidate School. Dorothy became pregnant. My brother Terry was born, the event marked by a printed announcement headed "Taillon Stampede" and listing the doctor in attendance as the Arena Judge and the nurses as Pickup Riders. Along with everyone else on their mailing list, I got this announcement and glued it into my scrapbook, beside clippings about my mother's bowling league. It was the first piece of mail from Cy for nearly a year.

Ila Mae wrote, full of goodwill toward the reconstituted Taillons and breathless about the baby. Cy was sorry now that he had named me after him, she said. Otherwise Terry could have been Cy Jr. Always practical, she suggested that since "Cyra funny name anyway as I have all ways said," the problem could be solved if Roy and Pat changed my name. Her suggestion was Minnie Mae, after my maternal grandmother, who was "living saint until God took her to be angel."

Longing to see the new baby, I got my chance at last. Cy was stationed in Oakland, California, and was coming home, briefly, to get Dorothy and Terry. He'd found an apartment, no easy task in

wartime. Before they left, he called and arranged
for me to visit the family in Great Falls. I went,
and through no fault of mine or anyone else's, became a burden on Cy and Dorothy's marriage that
both of them deeply resented. During that week,
Pat had her second nervous breakdown. This one
was so severe she was sent back to the hospital at
Warm Springs immediately.

Behind the closed doors I had learned to associate
with trouble, Cy talked to Roy on the telephone.
Afterward, in the upstairs bedroom of the Cosgriffs'
house, he and Dorothy shut themselves away for
hours, conferring over the crisis. The room was thick
with smoke from Cy's cigarettes, his remaining vice,
when he emerged to tell me that I was coming along
with him, Dorothy and Terry to Oakland. He had
the grace to tell me what was going on this time,
though I dimly understood "nervous breakdown."
Roy was too upset himself to take care of me, he
said. He also agreed with Cy that the cause of Pat's
illness was overwork. "She had to go and start another damned dance studio."

Several months before, Pat had launched "Patricia's School of the Dance" on the ground floor of a
moving and storage company in Missoula. It offered
tap, ballet and exercise classes for what ads forth-
rightly called "fatties" and was an instant success.

The money must have come from Roy, not a
large investment in that it involved only rent and
equipping the place with mirrors, ballet barres and
exercise mats. It must have been large to him, and

how my mother talked him into freeing her from her captivity, as well as backing her financially, I can't imagine.

That Cy was remarried may have had something to do with it, in that he no longer posed so grave a threat. It may have occurred to Roy that having married his dream woman, the glamorous show girl, he had turned her into a household drab. Hidden under a bushel, or one of Ila Mae's housedresses, Pat's light cast no luster on him. Whatever negotiations took place behind the scenes, Patricia's School of the Dance opened with fanfare.

The Daily Missoulian ran my mother's press release, the same one she'd used when she opened her Billings studio years before. It outlined her theatrical career, with flourishes, and included a high-minded statement about Dance and the Whole Child. We held an open house for prospective customers, with iced tea and bakery cookies. Old publicity pictures of Pat filled the big window facing the street: Pat in a feathered headdress doing the splits, Pat waving from the door of an airplane, "en route to further studies in Paris." Had she really been to Paris? I asked her, dying to hear all about it. That's what it said, didn't it? she snapped.

By the end of her first month, she had so many students, kids taking tap after school and their mothers sweating through acrobatic routines mornings and evenings, she had to hire an assistant instructor, a high school girl who had mastered the time step and could lead Beginning Tap, over and over, through "East Side, West Side."

Roy kept the books at the studio and spent all his evenings there. I reported to the place after school and ran errands, among them checking out library books on ballet for Pat. She knew virtually nothing about it but was teaching it anyway. Her students mainly learned to stand on one leg and point their toes.

I loved the school. One large bright room with a hardwood floor, it smelled of sweaty rubber mats and floor polish, the ammonia with which Roy and I cleaned the mirrors, and take-out food. With no time to go home for dinner, the three of us ate in the partitioned-off office at the front, on Roy's secondhand wooden desk. Though Roy claimed he went out for hamburgers and milk shakes only because no drive-ins offered take-out spinach, he loved the greasy food he preached was poisonous and fell on it with as much appetite as my mother and I did. Scratch a food faddist and you'll find a man whose erotic fantasies center on french fries.

Still slim and supple, no longer isolated from the world outside our bungalow, Pat turned into a beauty again. My mother was one of those women who can dazzle one day and the next look plain, gray-faced and lifeless. In retrospect, I can reconstruct the periods before her breakdowns by remembering how she looked. Light went out of her face a little at a time, as if behind her eyes she were pulling down a shade. As a child, I hadn't learned to read the signs and had no clue. So when her second bout of mental illness shattered her, life upended itself without warning. With my father and his new family, I left Great Falls in a few days, on a train packed tight with servicemen and headed for California.

The four of us had two seats. Dorothy sat in one holding Terry, whose restless crying rose up with the crying of other babies. I sat in the other, watching the landscape go by until the overhead lights dimmed and it was black outside. Cy stood for the whole trip in the crowded aisle, holding on to the overhead baggage rack and refusing to trade places with either Dorothy or me. His notion of chivalry dictated that he stand for eighteen hours or so while his wife and children sat.

My parents' shared-custody agreement, a cousin told me later, had resolved a deadlock. Neither parent wanted full-time responsibility for me. In fact, neither wanted custody. Cy wanted to pursue his rodeo career. Pat wanted to pursue the fantasy that she was still a show girl despite her marriage to Roy. They weren't enlightened but self-centered.

Wasn't that a fine kettle of beans? the cousin asked. Didn't it just make me want to shake the two of them until their teeth rattled?

Of course it did, but memory is selective. One couldn't live with it if it weren't. I prefer to remember my mother all dazzle and snap, leading her dancing classes at the studio while I gloried in gilt by association. I prefer to remember Cy swaying in the aisle on that trip to Oakland, gallant and asleep on his feet.

NINE

〰〰〰〰〰〰〰〰〰〰〰〰〰〰〰〰〰〰〰〰〰〰〰〰〰〰〰〰

The apartment in Oakland, dark and smelling of mildew, was in the basement of a stucco house on a hill. The rent for it was extortionate, Cy complained, wartime profiteering on the part of our landlady, who lived upstairs, scolded every time we turned on our radio, and threatened to evict us when I picked plums from the tree in the backyard. She didn't mind if they rotted unpicked, or if birds ate them, only if tenants' children did.

Without my being there, Cy, Dorothy and Terry would have been cramped in their three rooms. Cy's soldier's pay had to stretch farther than my father and his new wife anticipated. They had no privacy and countless practical problems, from putting me in school somewhere to getting along without a car, never easy in California. Because our hill was so steep, Dorothy could push Terry's buggy down it to shop, but not up again. She had to wait on the corner for Cy to come home on the streetcar, in the evenings, with her buggyload of baby, laundry and groceries.

Far harder on her, the apartment teemed with mice. Dorothy was in terror of them. I wasn't, and when she and I were at war with one another, I could always pretend that I had seen a mouse. It gave me a satisfying sense of power to see her standing on a kitchen chair, white-faced and help-less—my powerful stepmother reduced to power-lessness. She and I had quickly arrived at the relationship we never substantially altered. With equal vehemence, we detested each other.

So jealous of Cy she resented even the fraction of his affections I claimed, Dorothy was a setter of snares. In her version of our skirmishes, she made heroic efforts to please her stepdaughter. I failed to appreciate these efforts, or appreciate them enough, or appreciate them in the proper way, impossible because there was no proper way. "I'm not angry, I'm only hurt," was her litany.

"I'm not hurt, I'm only angry," I screamed back at her, and caught hell from my father for "sassing back." Like most men, Cy hated what he called "a cat fight," friction between women. His un-Solomon-like solution was to join in the shouting himself, until the landlady wielded her gavel, a broom handle, and brought us all to order by pounding on her kitchen floor, our kitchen ceiling.

Dorothy escalated our hostilities every chance she got. I became ever more resentful and cagier, as good at provoking her as she was at provoking me. She spent a lot of time on that kitchen chair, cowering from imaginary mice, and was subjected to worse forms of terrorism. Carrying the baby across the room, I got good at faking a stumble and making it look as if I were about to drop him on his head.

This hateful behavior I look back on without guilt because I was up against an equally unprincipled opponent. What affection I can find in my middle-aged self for Dorothy is based on what a worthy enemy she was, how determined and how inventive. I got up the Irish in her, she said, but what I really brought to flower in her was tactical genius. One has to respect the domestic Desert Fox who never deploys the same weapons in the same place or repeats the same maneuver.

I had few clothes with me in Oakland, only those I would have needed for a few days of visiting in Great Falls. Ila Mae's handiwork, these clothes were dowdy even at Our Lady of Lourdes, the Catholic school at the foot of the hill where Cy enrolled me. Other girls my age wore skirts and sweaters, he noticed, when he escorted me there on his way to the Army base in the mornings. I alternated among three skimpier versions of the housedresses Ila Mae made for Pat, cotton print sacks cut like those worn by early female missionaries. As tight as money was in the household, my fashion-conscious father insisted Dorothy buy me a pleated plaid skirt and matching sweater.

Dorothy set out on this mission alone. With unerring instinct, she picked out an outfit that made me look even more sallow and wizened than

I already looked, the skirt two sizes too large and so long it came to the top of my socks, the sweater a yellow-green never seen in nature, seldom in art. My skin took a greenish sheen from it even under the low-wattage light bulbs our landlady made us use.

Cy looked at me and registered the same despair he had felt when he paid ten dollars for a permanent wave and my hair didn't bend. His expression told me he had a hopeless case for a daughter: deck her out in a brand-new green sweater, and the whole kid turned green.

Dorothy told me how much these clothes had cost and the trial-by-streetcar she had gone through to buy them. All that money, and all that work, and one could tell from my sour look that I didn't like them. It just went to show that as far as I was concerned, she could do nothing right.

As soon as I put on that sweater and skirt, I knew they made me look like an organ grinder's monkey. I also knew it was politic to make a show of appreciation and launched into one fit for a cast of thousands. I jumped up and down, squealed, hugged Dorothy, hugged Cy, hugged Dorothy again. I said the skirt was the most beautiful skirt in the world and the sweater was even prettier. I claimed to want to sleep in these clothes, so that we would never be parted. Oh thank you thank you thank you thank you thank you. I concluded with a clog dance meant to convey wild excitement.

My stepmother watched. Her shoulders sagged and a pair of perfect tears spilled from her luminous green eyes. "You know," she said, "even if you don't like a present somebody gives you, you could pretend to be grateful."

That I remember this incident, so far in the past, is a sign of arrested development. I do remember it, and after thirty-five years, compulsively thank telephone solicitors for calling.

Our time in Oakland must have passed as slowly for Cy and Dorothy as it did for me. Cy was just one more lieutenant, and the man hated being one more anything. Dorothy, a gregarious young woman, was far from her friends and family, trapped in a basement with a new baby, a loathsome step-daughter and mice. Only Terry, blond, sunny-tempered and sturdy, thrived. The world's prize baby, in Cy's view, Dorothy's and mine, he made us into a family of sorts, in spite of ourselves, because we all thought of him as under our care and joint proprietorship. At Our Lady of Lourdes, I got into a fistfight with a girl who claimed her baby brother was walking before he was.

There, too, I was baptized as a Catholic at my own insistence. Frantic to conform, as usual, I had undergone a conversion of epic proportions, complete with religious visions lifted from *The Song of Bernadette* and an inner voice announcing I was destined to be a saint. When I wrote home about it, the baptism caused proportionate religious hysteria on my Aunt Ila Mae's part, and prompted one of the few letters Roy ever wrote me.

In his surprisingly elegant hand, he informed me that no matter how much holy water the priests and nuns had made me drink, I was a Lutheran. While he had no religious faith of his own, Roy knew all about "mackerel snappers" just as he knew all about house cats. Cats jumped on your chest and sucked out your breath while you were asleep. Catholics sucked out your soul, sold it on the soul market and turned the proceeds over to the Pope.

Ila Mae changed church affiliations frequently because she and the minister differed on some fine point of theology. Her restless quest stopped short of Catholicism, however, and she also wrote furious letters to Cy and Dorothy, more letters to me. In mine, she pointed out that Catholicism was for foreigners and I had been born right here in the U.S. of A.

I must have known that the Catholic Church and I were just one of those things, and that when I went back to Missoula, it would be all over between us. Certainly I threw myself into my new faith the way one hurtles into doomed love affairs, with such excessiveness the nuns at school were alarmed rather than pleased. I prayed for hours at a time, in front of the statues in the chapel; genuflected deeply upon entering and leaving the pews, as if taking a curtain call; told my rosary beads at recess and lunchtime, while everybody else ate. I had a brown-bag lunch but was fasting. No opportunity for a pietism got by me. I was ready with "Bless you" before anyone within miles thought of sneezing.

Though Cy looked at his prospective saint

askance too, he arranged for my baptism, and never one to miss an opportunity, asked his CO from the base to be my godfather. I do not remember that imposing gentleman's name because I never saw or heard from him again.

Because of my prayers, I felt sure at the time, the war finally ended. Cy took me to downtown Oakland, the streetcar we rode inching through the crowds in the street, to see the victory celebration. Confetti poured down on us from the tall buildings. Car horns blared. Men pounded my father on the back, because he was in uniform, and weeping women kissed him. Caught up in all that emotion, I had a satisfying cry too. Somewhere in the back of my mind was a release from the fear I had felt back in Missoula—that Cy would die in the war, that bombs would fall on the peaceful town, that there was no such thing as safety anymore, or sameness.

I was right about the "sameness" part. In a few weeks, I was back in Missoula again, my temporary family and I having made another long train ride home. And while Missoula was intact, not bombed into oblivion, my mother wasn't.

Though she'd been withdrawn sometimes before, I'd never seen her so old-looking and dispirited. She padded around the house in bedroom slippers, incurious about the time I had been away. Patricia's School of the Dance was empty, I could see through the dusty windows, except for the ballet barres that still lined the walls. No sign out front, no mirrors, no rubber exercise mats on the

floors. Roy must have sold the fittings secondhand
and closed the place while she was in the hospital
at Warm Springs.

At first I wondered if Pat missed the school, then
if she remembered that there had been one. She
moved around now in a fog of her own making,
smiling when she sensed that a response of some
description was called for, picking up small ob-
jects—ashtrays, copies of the *Reader's Digest*, pots
and pans—and then putting them back where she
got them. She seemed to be keeping herself busy,
but the busy work accomplished nothing and her
monotonous slow pacing led nowhere. Roy told me
to be nice to her and made an exhausted effort to
be nicer to her himself.

Why it takes so many years to forgive one's parents their failings and sympathize with their disappointments, I cannot explain. Nor do I know
why that sympathy comes so much harder than the
tolerance one summons easily for friends, or
strangers. All of Roy's long life, I thought of him
as a tyrant, my mother his helpless victim. Now I
know he was a victim of their marriage as much as
she was, a man who didn't miss the brass ring but
had the misfortune of catching it.

My stepfather must have lain awake nights, during those years, comparing the fantasy of Pat to
the damaged woman sleeping in the other room.
He must have felt he had two children, my mother
and me, neither one loving him and neither really
his. He was subject to night terrors, bad dreams

that made him cry out so loudly, I would get out of bed and wake him up.

To stall off the moment when I would leave him alone again, Roy told me about these nightmares in detail. Large animals sprang onto his back and dug their claws into him; no matter how he struggled, he could not shake them off. Gaping pits opened in front of the station wagon while he drove around Missoula replenishing vending machines. Someone close to him died, in dream after dream. Roy stood at the graveside, grieving deeply, but did not know who lay in the coffin.

From Wisconsin came word that his brother Vin actually had died, of bronchial flu. A sister wrote a long letter describing his last hours in the hospital and the funeral arrangements. "The casket was a very lovely one. The pillow was a sort of ashes of roses color and a third of the cover was too and a little in the scarf over the casket. You see he was so dark & thin we didn't want him to lay on white or cream."

Roy sat up all night, for a week, reading this letter over and over again. In the mornings, I'd find him in the same chair in the living room, the lights all on and cigarette smoke dense in the air. So superstitious he'd make a U-turn and drive around the block rather than let a black cat cross his path, my stepfather must have blamed himself for Vin's death, believed that his nightmares had been prophetic. If he fell asleep and dreamed the same dream again, someone else might die, one of

the few other human beings to whom he felt con-
nected.

What little he revealed of himself served only
to make him more opaque. We lived, when I was
ten years old, in a house that had two bedrooms
facing the street, North Avenue East. In mine one
winter evening, I sat on my bed reading, in my
Montgomery Ward catalogue mail-order underwear. Roy drove past, coming home from work,
hurtled into the house and my room and stood
there, still with his hat on, red-faced and wild-eyed.
On his forehead, a vein pulsed.

He snatched up a blanket and threw it over my
spindly form. "My God, woman," he shouted.
"*Are you mad?*"

What quirk of his sexual nature led him to see
a forty-pound child, in peach-colored cotton vest
and knickers, as Susanna tempting the elders?
What other quirk caused him to express his outrage in language that might have come from Edgar
Allan Poe? My stepfather remains as much a mys-
tery to me now as he was then, a man whose mind
resembled the curious hodgepodge he had created
in our basement.

I have a copy of a book he sold door to door in
1921, *The Standard Dictionary of Facts*. He must have
studied it extensively himself and had chosen to
underline "100 A.D., The Huns Migrate West-
ward" and "1834, Robert Peel, Premier, Difficulties
in Canada."

I have representative volumes from his library
on baldness remedies, cancer cures and the diag-

nostic talents of the lower bowel. Also heavily underlined is a book entitled *Making Yourself Taller*.

Though I have moved numbers of times myself, I have carted along Roy's canvas boxing shoes, in case I ever need them; a leather miner's apron and a Life Saver display rack from the candy company—useless artifacts, all of them, and impossible to discard. I keep expecting them to unravel for me that dour, inscrutable man who wanted to be taller, and hairier, and no doubt happier.

I leave him behind, for the moment, with his impracticable dreams and his night terrors, in order to catch up with Cy; but my stepfather will be back. Roy Qualley was tacked as closely to Cy Taillon's heels as his shadow.

TEN

~~~~~~

In 1945, after his discharge from the Army, Cy set out on the rodeo circuit again. He had promised Dorothy that when the war was over he would get a steady job, the kind that came with a regular paycheck, and that the family would settle down somewhere. No more gypsying; she had his word on it. In its place, security and a life that made sense.

He could no more have kept this promise than squeezed his feet into shoes without complaining that they pinched intolerably. My father was destined to announce rodeos the way other people are born cellists or water diviners. Keeping regular hours and leading a normal life, he would have vaporized, like the wicked witch in *The Wizard of Oz*, leaving nothing behind but gray ash and a pair of cowboy boots.

Whatever her preference in the matter, Dorothy went along with his change of heart, becoming an expert packer of suitcases, spending her evenings in motel rooms, with the baby, while Cy was at the fairgrounds orchestrating the roar of the crowd. Blessed with more sense than Pat had, she imposed the condition that Cy come straight home after the rodeo.

My newly respectable father did. For the first time in his life, he welcomed domesticity instead of finding ways to avoid it. He opened the first bank account he ever had and stayed out of the bars, which meant he had money to deposit in it.

That first year on the circuit after the war was as lean as the prewar years. Cy's itinerary for 1945 shows few bookings and entire weeks followed by the notation "To be announced at a later date."

He was on his way to a successful career notwithstanding. After 1946, and the Great Falls air show disaster, these itineraries run to three double-spaced pages, the rodeos so close together he had to fly, rather than drive, between some of them.

You can still hear firsthand accounts of this event over a whiskey ditch at the Cowboys Bar, across from the fairgrounds where it took place, and if you linger there long, you will. Calling itself a bar and museum, the Cowboys is lined with rodeo photos and populated with the former riders in them. These men, soft-bellied but with handshakes you can feel in your shoulder blades, reminisce about favorite Brahmas as if they were much-loved household pets. They also reminisce about what proved to be the turning point in my father's life on the circuit.

Pete Logan, another announcer, described it in

a tribute he wrote, for *World of Rodeo and Western Heritage*, when Cy retired. Noting that his long-time colleague "left indelible footprints along the long and lonely rodeo road," Logan tells what happened that afternoon in a style that suggests he would have also made a first-rate documentary filmmaker:

August, 1946. Great Falls, Mt. A hot August afternoon. Within seconds it got much hotter.

For some reason known only to God, the Air Force decided to fly three fully fueled airplanes past a grandstand that was occupied with no less than ten thousand people. An Air Force person was to comment on this as the rodeo waited. Without warning the planes collided. Bits and pieces of metal started falling. One plane ploughed into a race barn not three hundred yards from the grandstand and exploded, killing horses and people. A second one crashed into a hillside less than a quarter mile away and exploded. The third was able to stay airborne and stagger back to the Air Force base.

The Air Force person froze, unable to say a word. Cy immediately took over and calmly explained that there was no danger now. And as the heat from the burning plane, the awful smell of death permeated the atmosphere, the people remained pretty much as they were, transfixed at the horror of what they had seen.

The slightest suggestion of uncertainty or panic would have resulted in the death of scores of humanity. A then 17-year-old girl remembers bits of metal falling by her, with tiny sparks falling in her hair, the heat from the burning gasoline, and thru it all, hearing Cy talking to them.

Perhaps it was the same woman who told me her own version of this tale, a few summers ago, and in the course of it issued the definitive statement on Cy's voice. "I don't know what God looks like," she said, "but I know what He sounds like."

His presence of mind brought my father a citation from the Air Force and masses of publicity. Newspapers all over the country ran the story and his picture; intrigued with the strikingly handsome man with the profession no one outside the West had ever heard of, they also ran sidebars discovering rodeo. Bookings began to pour in, not just for rodeos but for public events of all kinds. After all the lean years of eating more dust than steak dinners, Cy was established.

At least he was established in most people's eyes. After the Great Falls air show disaster, he sent me a clipping. The story notes breathlessly: "In addition to his announcing experience he has been a theatrical producer, vaudeville performer, songwriter, dance musician, amateur boxer, airplane pilot and radio producer." Written beside this list is an addition only Roy Qualley could have made—"& Bum," it reads.

Westerners love a hero, and when the hero is one of their own, a cowboy, their pride does not diminish in a small matter of four decades. On trips back to Great Falls now, I size up the fairgrounds and wonder how such a small place could have held ten thousand people. I listen to eyewitness accounts of that afternoon and ponder their discrepancies. As the bourbon flows, the number of people killed increases, the explosion virtually wipes out Great Falls and my father remains at the mike while flames lick at the wooden announcer's stand.

I swallow my skepticism, along with the drink I am never allowed to pay for. As my father's daughter, I should know that mythmaking has its own logic.

I also know less about Cy, at that point in his life, than do the tale tellers, for just when he stepped to center stage, I drifted off into the wings and our long estrangement began. While I still joined Cy, Dorothy and Terry on the circuit from time to time, or spent a school holiday with them in Great Falls, I was never part of my father's household again after Oakland. As was inevitable, after his remarriage the father and the child of his first marriage began to grow apart.

Cy had two sons now, two future cowboys. My brother Tommy's birth in 1947 occasioned another announcement in the form of a mock rodeo program, reproducing the logo from Cy's letterhead. The Second Performance of the Taillon Stampede noted that Tommy Louis was the brother of the previous world champion baby boy, Terry James.

Along with the Arena Director, the Pickup Riders and the Judges (Cy's mother and father), this edition lists Mr. and Mrs. Cy Taillon as Producers and Cy Taillon as Announcer. Cy thus managed to get his own name in print twice.

He had his pretty second wife, who had transformed his life and made him infinitely happier. So domestic she made up motel beds in the mornings, with neat hospital corners, Dorothy was the wife my mother had refused to be, the woman behind the man instead of the one constantly stepping in front of him.

He had both the freedom of the road and a place to call home, the Cosgriff house in Great Falls. The family made its base there during the thirty days a year or so they weren't traveling.

Cy's voice boomed through that house and his proprietary presence filled it. His previous addresses had been boardinghouses, motels and favorite saloons. In Dorothy's mother's house, he enjoyed comforts ordinary to other people, extraordinary to Cy, such as beds without lumps in them, home cooking and full-sized bars of soap in the bathroom. His mail was waiting for him there, instead of bouncing from General Delivery in one town to General Delivery in the next.

Best of all, none of these things threatened to curb his independence because the house was not Cy's own. He could come and go, unencumbered by anything but his luggage. No one expected him to run errands or take down the storm windows; his arrival was an event, another personal appearance. My father never walked into a room, anywhere, without expecting faces to turn toward him and at least a silent round of applause. If one read a magazine when he was present, or listened to *Amos 'n' Andy* rather than to Cy, he sulked.

He knew no more drunken nights and unspeakable mornings. Nor did he start the day rummaging for enough change to put a few gallons of gas in the car. With his career thriving, Cy had become an astute businessman, acting as his own agent, commanding high fees. The first year he needed a tax accountant, he passed the news on to me, and thus to Pat and Roy, in Missoula. He was so busy now, he wrote, he could not keep track of his complicated financial situation.

Roy took the opportunity to deliver an address on the subject of Cy's unpaid child support. He never tried to collect this money, because he found it more satisfying that Cy owed it, but when Cy sent me a crisp new twenty-dollar bill for Christmas, Roy placed a personal lien on it. He opened a passbook savings account for me, at the First National Bank in Missoula, and soon had cause for more anger and indignation. No banking laws prevent minors from drawing their money out of savings accounts and investing it in Fred Astaire movies.

I would have preferred one of Cy's old Christmas boxes, full of stuffed olives and animal crackers. Cy didn't know about this because we knew less and less about each other. When I came to visit him, infrequently, we were taken aback by how the other had changed and how the familiar had become strange.

As I grew, I stayed thin and became gawkier, the kind of preadolescent poltergeist who can't move about without tripping over her own feet. From across a room, I could cause Dorothy's Hummel figurines to fall off their shelves. My hands were too big for the rest of me and hung at the ends of my wrists like a pair of empty gardening gloves. They were shaped like Cy's meticulously manicured hands, but his were deft, while what I did with mine, mainly, was drop things.

Immune to the sulfurous-smelling anti-acne cream Dorothy bought me, I broke out in blotches; was a demonstration model of nervous tics and twitches; still cried when spoken to sharply. In Cy's view, accurate in this case, I was also freakishly bookish. Normal twelve-year-old girls, by way of making conversation, did not recite "Hiawatha." After I confessed to Terry, who blew the whistle on me out of astonishment, that I had always been afraid of horses, my father knew no blood ties existed between us. My strongest memory of him then is Cy staring at me, with his heavy black eyebrows raised. He must have been trying to figure out who I was.

He seemed as alien to me. For years, Cy shared with champion bronc rider Casey Tibbs the title "World's Best-Dressed Cowboy." This accolade, awarded him by the Western Clothiers Association, my father earned with his wardrobe of dozens upon dozens of cowboy hats: soft grays and beiges, black, white and mossy green. Twenty color-coordinated outfits accompanied him on the road, Western suits made for him by a tailor in Denver out of fine, lightweight gabardine. Dorothy packed them all in layers and layers of tissue paper, so they emerged from suitcases without a wrinkle. His cowboy boots were also custom-made, of kangaroo skin. Cy had found that kangaroo skin was the softest of leathers, he told reporters. Now he could wear nothing else.

His shirts crackled with starch when they emerged from their own tissue-paper clouds. He held his tie in place with a diamond horseshoe stickpin fashioned from his mother's wedding ring. His best kangaroo-skin boots had gold- and silver-inlaid heels, and a leather hanging bag made for him by a fan had his profile at the mike tooled into it and the legend "Cy Taillon, World's Greatest Rodeo Announcer." Even his tuxedos, he told the Denver *Post*, were custom-tailored and Western-cut. The former peacock in the bright satin shirts had adopted his own version of quiet good taste.

At the curb in front of the Cosgriff house was the latest of his Buick Roadmasters. By 1959, Cy was driving 65,000 to 80,000 miles a year. By 1971, he had worn out nine of these cars as well as ten Cadillacs. Before he announced his last rodeo, he had put another half dozen cars out to pasture—in Western parlance, tuckered out.

One of these Roadmasters was salmon pink and silver, with my father's initials on silver plaques on the doors. At thirteen, I took it for a spin around the block, at his insistence, and almost put us both through the windshield when I stepped on the power brakes. Cy said I drove like my mother and asked if she had put me up to killing him.

He was a fixture, by then, at all the big rodeos with the romantic names, the Snake River Stampede, the Pike's Peak or Bust Rodeo, the American Royal Horse Show and the Calgary Stampede, as well as thirty smaller ones a year. By the late fifties, he estimated that 87,000 people had heard him announce. When he began presiding over rodeos on national television, the number shot up, and he received requests for signed photos, as if he were a movie star.

Announcing in Madison Square Garden, he even impressed an eastern sportswriter and got a good if condescending review, one that suggested he was not as provincial as New Yorkers might expect: "His diction is excellent and he speaks gentlemanly English with a faint touch of Westernism."

We went nowhere, when I traveled with the family, where my father was not lionized and where people did not crowd around him, dogging his gold and silver heels and hanging on his every word. To these people's amazement, he remembered all their names from one year to the next, cowboys, local rodeo officials, fans and, without exception, reporters. No wonder it irritated Cy that I would not wear cowboy boots anymore; that I'd as soon watch television in the motel as sit through every performance he gave; that when I did go, while he enthralled the rest of the rodeo crowd, I sat in the grandstands and read.

Out of necessity, I had ceased to be a satellite spinning in his orbit. So there he was, with his rodeo-loving sons, his tireless press agent of a wife and a daughter who looked like him, was named after him and had decided "seen one rodeo, you've seen them all."

Public speakers always find themselves preoccupied with the face in a crowd stretched into a yawn. Mine must have been that bored face Cy picked out, blandly disengaged except when a calf got its neck broken in the calf-roping event.

On these occasions, infrequent though they were, I registered moral outrage. Rodeo was cruel, I said. This attitude my father could not tolerate, not from me, not from journalists and, most of all, not the self-righteous, lily-livered SPCA.

Cy no longer "cussed." He made an exception for misguided critics of the sport that was his life as well as his livelihood. In a piece he wrote for *Western Horseman*, he tells of trying to convert some SPCA officials, at a rodeo in Chicago, "to my honest belief that any cruelty in the game applies more to the contestants than to the stock." Bucking horses did not work over five minutes a year and "enjoyed the greatest freedom of any animal." Thousands of calves and steers "were slaughtered every day, without a sporting chance, in order to provide meat for our tables . . ." As for injuries, "a ratio of about ten contestants were injured for any animal hurt in any way."

Soon after the Chicago rodeo began, a quarter horse burst out of the chute without a buck-jump.

"Attaining great speed, it veered sharply to the left and exploded into the concrete wall from which it rebounded with an obviously broken neck: With tongue lolling grotesquely, the animal gave a few convulsive jerks and was dead."

From the crow's nest, the Voice of the West announced that this animal was merely stunned. "I also expressed the hope that it would soon recover."

The audience, including the SPCA inspectors, was not convinced. It booed and hissed. Cy ducked behind the chutes for a desperate consultation with the stock producers.

The dead horse had been dragged out of the arena, in full view of the hostile crowd. Later in the rodeo, notwithstanding, my father announced that it had been "frightened or confused by the lights" and was once again in perfect health. Into the arena charged a similar horse, flummoxing the Chicagoans, who couldn't tell one horse from another. "We went on to complete one of the most enthusiastically received performances of the entire engagement."

My rodeo heritage aside, my heart still goes out to the steer when the rope snaps taut around its neck. I wince when the rider jumps from his horse, runs down the rope and twists its neck in a hammerlock. But I have come to accept the sport on its own terms and keep my remaining objections to myself. Call this craven if you will. Then ponder what might have happened to a daughter of Manolete, at the bullring in Madrid, who was moved to wail, "Oh, the poor bull."

ELEVEN

In an old "Red Ryder" cartoon panel, the strip's creator, Fred Harmon, has Red say to Cy Taillon, "It wouldn't be a show without your silver-tongued palaver." I'm sure my father liked the exposure and that he took exception to the word "show." A major concern of his, as he refined and developed his style at the mike, was that rodeo develop a more dignified image as well. It was a sport, not a carnival act, and it behooved everyone who had anything to do with it—sportswriters, fans and contestants alike—to remember that.

Bronc riders and record-time ropers, a modest lot, rarely wave their hats at the crowd or give each other "high fives" at the end of a ride. Any who did would have felt the cutting edge of Cy's silver tongue.

The reporter who wrote about colorful buckaroos putting on a daredevil Wild West show soon had a wrathful Cy on the other side of his desk, his expensive boots parked on it and his voice making the paper clips rattle. Rodeo belonged on the sports page, not in the entertainment section, and the correct term was "rodeo athletes," not "cowpokes."

The fan who caught up with him to tell him he and the wife thought those hands sure could ride was set straight. Rodeo contestants were not ranch hands but professional riders and ropers. "They have developed such skill with rampaging livestock," Cy thundered at a writer for a Fort Worth newspaper, "that the average ranch hand would be licked hands down in competition with them." Putting an ordinary ranch hand in the rodeo arena, in fact, would be like "letting a sandlot baseball player in the World Series."

The writer had said in print that cowboys were cowboys, not athletes. When my father got through with him, he published a follow-up column deciding that he "just possibly was wrong."

Cy wore the Western equivalent of Savile Row tailoring because he wanted to look like a man presiding over a major sports competition rather than like a barker for Annie Oakley or Wild Bill Hickok. He pioneered the "straight man" style of announcing, even when the cowboys themselves told him he sounded like a storefront lawyer, because he thought the old style of cornball comedy from the crow's nest was an affront to both competitors and audience. Says Pete Logan, who began announcing rodeos the year after Cy did, "At times he was stubborn, uncompromising and difficult, but always a dedicated professional. He was acutely aware that his conduct and appearance reflected on our profession." Thus he set standards that those who followed him had to have "if they ever expected to get out of the bushes."

Much of the impetus for these reforms, I am certain, came from Dorothy, who turned Cy into a gentleman by being a lady, unmistakable as anything but one, in a world that divided women into two categories. One was what my brother Terry calls "twinks, scuzzbutts and squirrels," rodeo groupies. The other was good ol' gals, female counterparts of their Western men.

Good ol' gals wore jeans and boots. They hauled horse trailers as handily as they hauled their husbands from a bar, or someone else's bed, and had what Dorothy called "mouths on them." They could tell dirty stories, drink men twice their body weight under the table or ride a breakneck barrel race.

Dorothy stuck to dresses and high-heeled shoes, though there are no heels high enough to traverse a rodeo grounds and end up smelling like a rose. She never laughed at a dirty joke, much less told one, and had a way of causing the joke teller to wither and mutter, "No offense intended." In her mink-stoled and perfumed wake, gentility followed, trotting to keep up.

So did the old-fashioned gallantry cowboys accord "ladies" and grudging deference from members of her own sex. Somehow my stepmother spent her long married life on the circuit without its rough-and-tumble rubbing off on her. Instead, she rubbed the rough-and-tumble off the circuit, and Cy. It was a point of pride with her that the house the family eventually bought in Denver showed "no trace of any Western influence." Neither did Dorothy, she emphasized to an interviewer in Sydney, Australia, where Cy announced the riding events at the Royal Easter Show. While she professed to love rodeo, she disliked Western dress, would never wear it and made only one concession to it. This was to wear clothes made in the same fabric as her husband's suits. "The dress I wear merely complements his outfit."

No cowboys bunked on the wall-to-wall carpet in that house in the suburbs of Denver. My father's collection of Western bronzes was consigned to the den. It could have been the house of a branch bank manager or a dentist.

The sport was changing along with Cy, rubbing off its rough edges. Back in 1945, a group of rodeo contestants had founded the Cowboys Turtle Association, so named because they had been so slow in seeing the need for it and getting it started. The organization was a union of sorts, its intention to cut riders and ropers in on a fair share of the profits.

Before the Turtles, promoters could stage rodeos and skip out with the gate. Contestants' entry fees were not added to the prize money for an event; the cowboy paid for the privilege of risking life and limb, while the promoters scooped in both his entry fees and the money fans paid to pass through the turnstiles.

The organization became the Rodeo Cowboys Association and eventually the Professional Rodeo

Cowboys Association, which now regulates all phases of the rodeo profession. One of its rules is that entry fees must be added to the prize money. Though he may have to enter ninety or a hundred rodeos a year, sometimes competing in two on the same day, a top cowboy can keep himself in Holiday Inns, Levi's and orthopedic surgeons. If he's a champion, and his kids don't insist on enrolling in rodeo school in Henryetta, Oklahoma, or Clovis, California, an all-American bronc rider can put them through Yale.

These gains came hard, over the objections of the producers. The producers hired Cy and issued his contracts—more often than not, in the form of a handshake—and signed his paychecks. Because his sympathies were with the cowboys, he joined the RCA anyway and promoted it from the beginning. One cowboy who approved wrote the following poetic tribute: "Cy Taillon tossed his Stetson aside / And kissed the girls goodbye. / This is one big show he can't announce, / But he's workin' it high."

Numbers of more formal testimonials followed. Over Cy's desk, in later years, was a display of awards, including one from International Rodeo Management naming him the 1966 "Rodeo Man of the Year." My father rode tall in the saddle in the eyes of money men and cowboys alike.

How could we find common ground anymore, when he became such an estimable personage, his daughter and the Voice of Rodeo? Never a shy wood violet, Cy now took himself seriously indeed. He became an avatar of traditional American values and a pre–Ronald Reagan symbol of political conservatism. He grew cocksure of his judgment even when it made little or no sense, as when, though a Republican, he voted for John F. Kennedy "to show that Catholics aren't prejudiced."

He claimed intimacy with the rich and powerful, beginning sentences with "When I went fishing with Ike Eisenhower last summer . . ." or "I've been in touch with Lyndon about that, and he told me confidentially . . ." His name-dropping made me writhe. So did Dorothy's claim, in the press, that my father's most notable characteristic was his modesty.

In Denver, he ran a Captain Queeg–like tight ship. All hands on deck for an early breakfast, permission to go ashore viewed with suspicion, liberties canceled for infractions. As what I still think was a mildly rebellious adolescent, I managed to break every rule in his book when I was around and inspire the issuing of new ones. Cy once woke me out of a sound sleep to point out my lack of consideration for others, in the form of a single hair in the sink.

No one is purer in thought, word and deed than a reformed rakehell. No one is as insufferable. Cy now expected hero worship, but he was not going to get it from me, and what he got instead were reminders that I had known him for a long time and did not look upon him as a candidate for Mount Rushmore.

Nor had time altered my relationship to my old antagonist, Dorothy. No longer the insecure young woman I thought of as my wicked stepmother, she was still doing a convincing imitation. She had gained weight, had a matronly quality now and dyed her hair its former auburn. What had not changed was that she still resented my existence, as evidence of my mother's existence. In actuality, she explained to me once, I didn't exist.

She reasoned as follows. Cy was Catholic. My mother wasn't. If Cy had married outside the Church, he hadn't really married. If there was no first marriage, there could be no child born of it.

With the test of this syllogism standing there, living, breathing and marveling, some accommodation had to be made. It stopped short of the reality principle. I think my stepmother convinced herself that my attachment to the Taillons was the result of a mix-up in the record-keeping procedures of Deaconess Hospital.

With Terry and Tommy, I was on more tolerant ground. They thought me prissy. I considered them a pair of roughnecks. We formed close ties despite all this, probably because they too were riddled with faults, and heard about them. Scatter them thousands of miles apart, and the children of the same family remain an affinity group. Growing up, always, is a matter of "us against them," and in relation to Dorothy and Cy, my brothers and I were the "us."

All three of us were proud of our father and longed for his good opinion. All of us fell short of his standards and ignited his short fuse. I fought him with words, the torrents I could produce as part of his genetic legacy to me. As a teenager, Terry once fought him physically.

Coming in late one night, he found his small, stainless-steel father waiting for him in the kitchen. The two enacted the universal father/son scene: Where have you been? You've got your mother worried half to death.

Strapping teenage son: She can go to hell . . .

Cy escorted Terry out to the backyard to discuss their differences. He had not lost his skills as a Golden Gloves boxer. Says Terry, "The next thing I knew, I was on my back, looking at the stars. He really Powder Rivered me."

According to the code of the West, one does not disparage motherhood, or its embodiment, Mother. Whatever the law in the rest of the land, we lived under that code, with Cy keeping a boot on the back of the neck of the lawless element. He revised the code as he went along but never its underlying tenet: thou shalt honor thy father the rodeo announcer, or encounter his ire, backed up, if necessary, by one hell of a punch.

He was impossible, I thought then, a tyrant. I still think so but give him credit for consistency.

My mother had done battle with Cy toe to toe, as incendiary-tempered as he was and as fond of a good brawl. Far more intelligent than Pat was, Dorothy employed guerrilla tactics, tears and wounded feelings. These always won the day because Western men hold the unexamined belief that they "can't stand to see a woman cry."

They believe this about themselves because they

learned it from their mothers. For the same reason, they believe that women are the weaker sex, that men are their strong protectors and that a man's house or mobile home is his castle. These inculcated attitudes leave Western women a lot of room to wield the power behind the saddle, without appearing to come anywhere near it. My stepmother knew this intuitively, and in her traditional femininity, her furs, bangles and beads, must have been more terrible to Cy than an army with banners. You can't challenge a lady to come out and fight like a man.

I fought with my father because I wasn't a lady, I was a teenager and thus a rolling gland. I fought with him because while I did not miss Cy the reckless drunk, I missed the Cy who had been fallible. I fought with him because he was bigoted against Jews, blacks, Easterners, intellectuals, hippies, draft resisters, Democrats, city dwellers and sopranos.

I liked to listen to opera on the radio. Cy called it "caterwauling" and imitated the female singers in falsetto.

The more he believed his own press, and saw himself as exemplar of the best of America, the more he railed against what he saw as the worst, anything that did not fall within the narrow confines of his values. What was most maddening was that he thought of himself as the model of tolerance, some of whose best friends were hippie Jewish sopranos. Arguing with him was tilting at a windmill of rectitude, and one always ended up unhorsed. Over the telephone, my father once drove me into an incoherent, stuttering rage. He waited it out and asked me if there were psychiatrists in Missoula.

Cy's politics and his all-round conservatism were not unusual in his part of the world and still aren't. In a coffee shop in Montana just a few years ago, I heard one man in cowboy boots tell another that England ought to "stop pussyfooting around and bomb the living shit out of the Falklands."

I leaned over the leatherette booth between us and asked why. He told me that you had to stop the Commies somewhere, little lady, and apologized for having said "shit."

I knew I was home, and felt the same mixture of helpless affection and anger I often felt toward Cy. Most people live with vacillation and doubt. Men like my father have no doubts and never vacillate: the natural order of things is as clear to them as their favorite trout streams, or the Rocky Mountain air, and on the cloudiest day, they can still see forever.

What Cy saw was a landscape of immutable certainties, one I have sometimes longed to rest my eyes upon as he did. Always seeing himself as acted upon, rather than acting, he was a stranger to the paralyzing emotion I know best, vague, all-purpose guilt. I drag quantities of it around, like a suitcase full of bricks. My father once spelled out his version of self-blame in a letter to me.

He was not only at odds with me just then but disappointed in my brothers. "I am probably unfortunate," he wrote, "in being a most sensitive person and having an all encompassing love for those I had a part in creating."

I stopped visiting Cy. He stopped visiting and calling me. He collected more accolades, and made more money, and became still better known. I went about my own life, reading about him more often than I saw him. For source material I had the private museum for which my stepfather Roy served as curator, the mentions of Cy that came over the teletype machines at *The Daily Missoulian*, where I was known as a copyboy, and the clippings Ila Mae sent.

In our Missoula house was a large wooden desk where no one ever wrote a check or affixed a stamp to a letter; its function was to serve as one more hollow log where Roy could stuff things. In its drawers, along with thousands of pipe cleaners, a massive collection of No. 2 pencils and, eventually, thirty-seven years' accumulation of unopened junk mail, Cy's onetime best pal stuffed articles torn out of magazines and every scrap of print about Cy he could get his hands on.

He pushed these into the backs of the drawers, burying them under the pipe cleaners. I rummaged for and found them. Such was the strength of Roy's mysterious obsession that he kept tracking Cy long after I left home, tearing the one-line listing out of *TV Guide* when Cy announced rodeos on national television, unconsciously imitating Cy by underlining my father's name.

The great river of letters Ila Mae wrote, going for the record in Sheer Volume of Personal Correspondence, had Cy as their major subject—every sighting in Great Falls, every bit of malicious gossip she could glean from unnamed sources. "Heard something wrong with Cy, he losing His Voice. Their trying to keep it hush but he in trouble now. The paper said he was taking vacation, he really have operation at the Mayo Clinic."

My mother seemed to have forgotten Cy at last, as she had forgotten so much else, but as his status as living Western legend grew, no one else who'd ever met him seemed immune to my father's fascination. Even my high school teacher collected clippings for me, asked to be introduced to him someday and told me how they'd heard him, sometime, somewhere, and never forgotten his mighty Wurlitzer voice.

My sense of his powerfulness increased, and my determination not to become fixed on him, ever again, as the pole star. Not only had that misconception caused me pain in the past, I could see its effects on my mother.

The large Taillon family boasts a great many cousins, one of whom has her own theory about why my father and I quarreled so long and bitterly and why, after I was fifteen or so, I had to take his all-encompassing love for his children on faith. Her reason is less cerebral than mine are.

"Don't you know what you did to cross Cy?" my cousin Sis asked me. "All of a sudden, you shot up and got taller than he was."

Roy Qualley as a young man in Great Falls, Montana.

To my Dear Wife Pat
May all our days be
as happy as this one   Love Roy
10-19-41

LEE STUDIO
OCONTO, WIS.

The photo of himself that Roy gave Pat on their
wedding day—and later tore in half.

Pat, Cyra and Roy in Missoula, Montana.

Ila Mae and Pat on an icy sidewalk during one of
Ila Mae's frequent visits to Missoula.

PAXSON SCHOOL GRADES 5-6 '48

Cyra (first row, second from left) in her skinned-back-pigtails stage.

Dorothy Cosgriff in her high school years.

Cy, Tommy, Dorothy and Terry on the road between rodeos.

Cyra in Missoula at about age twelve.

A teenaged Cyra leaning against the Buick Roadmaster
in front of the Cosgriff family home, 1954.

Cy Taillon, "World's Greatest Rodeo Announcer."

TWELVE

It took him twenty years, but my father finally managed to arrange an annulment of his marriage to my mother, thereby ratifying his long, stable marriage to Dorothy. Pat had been a youthful mistake. Dorothy was the helpmeet and full-time companion for whom Cy always came first, and my father adored her.

She traveled the circuit with him, though it meant leaving Terry and Tommy, whom she also loved with fierce possessiveness, in the charge of housekeepers much of the year. She selected his clothes, color-coordinating them as relentlessly as she did her own. Without complaint, she lived out of suitcases and motel rooms, spent the rest of her time in automobiles, traveling the same roads year after year, and became as skilled a promoter of Cy's business interests as he was.

Typical of their marriage was that my stepmother never learned to drive. She merely came along in the passenger seat while Cy steered their joint course. Even Ila Mae approved of her vocation as the woman behind the man and expanded on it in one of her treatises on marriage. "I always say it important for man to be king, thats the way it has always been with Wiley and Me, for God created he woman out of mans rib. The man came first Remember That Pat."

Her attitude would have come as news to Wiley, but he wrote no letters and issued no rebuttals. Instead, he spent his days trying to become invisible, keeping his nose in the sports pages, his feet off the ottoman and his head off the crocheted doily over the back of the chair. If he left shoe-polish smudges on the upholstery and hair-oil stains on the doilies, it wasn't for lack of trying to pass through his own household without a trace.

My uncle sought not earthly rewards, nor pie in the sky when he died, but domestic tranquillity. He might as well have aimed at being the first men's clothing salesman on the moon. His hundred-pound spouse had the stamina of a jockey, the eye-hand coordination to snatch a speck of dust out of the air before it settled on one of her end tables and an insatiable appetite for reform. In this, the world stubbornly continued to defy her, going its own untidy way. Crime raged in the streets. Promiscuity grew rampant. Drugs ravaged America's youth. Wiley shed cigarette ash on the carpet.

Ila Mae wrote on, her pen the weapon she wielded against chaos. Her stream-of-consciousness prose reveals her vision of the interconnectedness of all things, sometimes with alarming clarity.

"Two young girls were robbed & stabbed here that worked at the taco treat, they caught the men. One blessing they didn't rape them. Know what I would do if I got my Hands on them, Wiley have cold he leave filthy Kleenex all over the Place."

All the years he had been married to my mother, Ila Mae thought of Cy as the Prince of Darkness. Now that he was successful, and happily remarried, and no longer a drunk, his former sister-in-law reinstated him back into the human race, and ever magnanimous, appointed herself his best friend and spiritual adviser.

My father rarely called her and never went to see her. She interpreted his neglect as proof of their indissoluble bond, intimacy so profound it threatened Dorothy. "Cy was here and he didn't come to see me, guess Dorothy wouldn't let him. Her sister say he always asks about me. For he know I always have good cup of coffee for him if he need somebody to talk to." She had advice ready to serve up with the cream and sugar. Dorothy should stop dying her hair, Cy was ruining his feet in those cowboy boots and my brothers were going to end up in jail if he did not stay home with them more often. Teenage hoodlums were the product of "broken homes."

Cy never came around to profit from this wisdom. It accumulated, doing no one any good, until Ila Mae bundled it off to us in Missoula. She must have known her constant reminders of Cy caused unrest in our household but attributed to herself only the purest of motives. "Know Susie would want to know about Cys throat, she could send him a get well card & maybe a letter."

I'm sure my mother did not want to be reminded of Cy at all, or to hear about Dorothy, the paragon. Roy could have taken no pleasure from Ila Mae's description of Cy's house in Denver, which she had never seen but described as rivaling the Taj Mahal. Her misinformed medical bulletins upset me and got Roy's hopes up until Cy turned up on television again, the voice as sonorous as ever, the man as dapper and handsome. When it came to malicious mischief, my law-and-order aunt was a repeat offender.

Cy and I lived at such physical and emotional distance from one another by then that I knew almost as little about him as Ila Mae did. My visits were occasions for friction, my view of my father the blinkered view of an adolescent in revolt against a parent who overwhelmed me. Terry and Tommy knew another Cy entirely, and loved him so much less critically, their adult lives are memorials to him.

I found him heavy-handed on the reins, and bucked, and reared, and finally bolted out of his reach. My brothers found in him the model of a Western man, with the perfect mix of toughness and tenderness, and as soon as they were old enough, took to the circuit as rodeo cowboys. They knew his hard anger too, but looked upon it as strength; could have chosen lives outside the rodeo but never considered it; believe that while none of us can ever measure up to our father's stature, we were privileged to see the mark made on the wall.

The father Terry and Tommy grew up with instructed them in the deft and serene art of fly fishing. He taught them to put out a line as lightly as a sigh and to smell a trout swimming in some dark eddy, smugly assuming it is going to die of old age. He spent their thousands of hours on the road together teaching them about wildlife. Both my brothers can spot a mountain goat on a mountain-goat-colored rocky promontory or an eagle so high overhead it looks like a wren. Accurate within a few hours, they can predict the first snowflake of winter from the quality of a chill in the air.

Both are dead shots. Though Cy's passion was fishing, he saw to it they learned to hunt, because in Montana hunting is not only a rite of manhood but a means of filling the larder. At a cousin's house in Billings a few years ago, the dinner entrée was antelope tacos. Terry had shot the antelope, and split an elk with a hunting buddy the past winter, and took great glee in telling me what I was eating. He was reminding the sister from San Francisco who she really was and where she really came from. The antelope tacos were good but greasy. We washed them down with quarts of orange soda pop.

Tommy stores Cy's files, his scrapbooks and copies of the articles he wrote for Western publications. In them our father reminisced about favorite horses, adventures on the rodeo circuit and his love for wild birds. Sentimental articles, written in Cy's literate, ornate style, they brought him more recognition and more fan letters. My brothers tell me that the wild birds he wrote about ate out of Cy's hand.

We are children of the same man, the three of us, but of different memories, and when we're together now, we spend much of our time trying to make those memories mesh, living testimony to the staying power of his presence. The public Cy looms as large, still written about frequently years after his death.

That Cy, the rodeo announcer, never missed an engagement. In health or shaking in his boots with a fever, he turned up at the microphone and routinely gave a performance that earned a standing ovation. As an especially lyrical reporter put it, "He can fairly make you hear the cling-clang of spurs, the snap of leather, the furious snorting of the bronc demons as they come kicking, leaping, swirling out of the chutes defying any man to stay aboard."

The remarkable part of this description is that Cy made the reporter hear all these things in a newspaper office, a week in advance of the show.

Long after he became successful, he would drive all night to appear at a small-time rodeo because his being there guaranteed a crowd. Cy said he chose his profession because he wanted to be his own boss. In reality, he worked for the sport he loved, so slavishly that he rarely took time off.

He caught colds working in downpours in roofless announcer's booths, sweated in heat waves without loosening his tie or taking off his jacket and went out to the fairgrounds two hours before a performance to study his program notes, intent on coordinating the flow of events seamlessly. There he also made rounds, shaking hands with veteran cowboys, meeting the green kids riding in their first rodeos and wishing them luck. His compendious memory tucked away their names and histories. The green cowboy plummeted out of the chute on a bronc demon to the sound of Cy's voice, introducing him as glowingly as if he were a champion.

His closest rival for the rodeos that meant big money and prestige was Pete Logan, whom Cy respected as another dignified professional. Cy never tried to move into Logan's territory, Logan wrote, though "he has had several chances at me I am sure." Not only would doing so have been unethical, but "Cy [never] tried to replace anybody that was doing his job."

The onetime rounder had become principled, hardworking and reliable, a man whose handshake was as good as his signature on a contract. If he seemed pompous to me, swollen beyond recognition with pride, he would have argued he had earned that pride. The early years of Cy's life were a trajectory toward crash and burn, alcoholic drifting and a marriage that threatened to destroy him with its violent emotional extremes. He climbed out of the rubble determined never to look back.

From my vantage point as part of my father's past, I resented the extent of that resoluteness. I might have been more sympathetic to it had I been able to look upon my mother's course as its alternative. Though she functioned more or less normally for periods of weeks or months, by the time I was in high school the fogs closed in again without warning. Pat wandered off into them, in the clutch of private misery that put her out of Roy's reach and mine. During one of these withdrawals, she dug her old, cracked Samsonite suitcase out of the basement, packed it with odds and ends of her clothing and sat in a chair, waiting, as if the Missoula house were the Milwaukee Railroad depot downtown, near her former School of the Dance, and she were ready to go wherever the next train would take her. She came out of her lassitude to struggle with Roy when he took the suitcase away from her, more roughly than was necessary.

From Great Falls, Ila Mae assumed responsibility for her medical care, genuinely concerned about Baby Sister, taking her usual pleasure in a crisis. She pelted us with the names of doctors and clinics, legal expertise—"There would be no public hearing no one would have to know about it, just be signed by a Judge"—and pep talks urging Pat to cooperate in her own healing. "The treatment have to be given in closed ward hospital where they have special trained nurses for it . . . so Pat don't you think if you could be cured six weeks would be worth it . . . Some times we have to do things we don't want to."

My mother's breakdowns embarrassed Roy, as did all information about the family that became known outside it, lumped together as "washing your dirty laundry in public." He waited the latest

illness out, forbidding me to talk about it, raging
and weeping if it went on long. I marched back
and forth to school and to my job at *The Daily
Missoulian*, removing myself from a situation I felt
powerless to change, protected by my own isolat-
ing fog. Ila Mae scolded. And scolded.

"Dr. Layne is a very brilliant man & he has
gone out of his way to be helpful in this case. Roy,
bring her, I would take her my self, I could do all
the talking for her."

I don't think Roy ignored my aunt so much as
he no longer heard her. Too many letters, over too
many years, fell through the mail slot in our front
door twice a day, filled every crevice in the house
and exceeded his capacity to absorb them. Roy was
like a soldier in combat who had learned to sleep
through machine-gun fire.

Trivial or consequential, Ila Mae's letters are one
long letter, really, no installment ever complete.
She folded up her sheaf of blue-lined sheets, put
all those words in an envelope and sealed it. Irre-
sistible impulse seized her, and on the outside of
it, she scribbled a recipe: "One can potato soup
condensed, 1 can milk, handfull of cheese cheddar,
mix well, shredded wheat, bake. I serve with jello
mold fruit cocktail in it."

We heard about every head cold, every dish Ila
Mae washed and every insight that came to her as
she struggled to make sense of human existence: "I
always say God have a plan," she wrote when she
had some painful dental work done. "My gumbs hurt
so bad today tho don't ask me what it is."

We knew about every change in the weather in Great Falls, Montana, over forty years. Ila Mae took blizzards as personally as she took holdups at the Taco Treat, as visitations upon her by a malevolent universe.

When the spring thaws came, she raised her voice in seasonal rhapsodies. The crocuses pushed through the ground, the birds sang and her arthritis no longer troubled her. "This winter so long I thought God trying to kill me."

Her never-ending letter testifies to the need to chronicle one's life, lest its events have no significance beyond oneself, and the trouble with them is that in our household they turned into cries of "Wolf!" so familiar they lost the power to mobilize the villagers.

Ila Mae's health preoccupied her, the migraine headaches that run in the family, arthritis and a painful chronic ailment described only as "My Colon." As frequently as she switched from one church to another, she went from doctor to doctor. Her search wasn't for one who could cure her as much as it was for the one doctor who would understand how much she suffered, who would set aside whole afternoons for her visits and pick up his telephone each and every time she called.

"I in Hell and He out playing golf," she wrote when one doctor defected from his full-time responsibility. She intended to sue him, because, for once, she wasn't going to take it lying down.

The woman downstairs would testify in court that she'd seen Ila Mae that day looking half dead. Ila

Mae had demanded her medical records, which would have kept the few copying machines in Great Falls busy until both plaintiff and defendant had died of old age. A new doctor took the place of the target of her wrath and created a diversion. He performed surgery on My Colon, apologizing on behalf of the entire medical profession that it hadn't been performed long ago. My aunt wrote that "they took out practically the whole Thing." The fragment remaining still hurt, though not as much as that source of indescribable torture, her bridgework.

Roy telephoned Wiley, while Ila Mae was in the hospital, and sent flowers that "set him back" ten dollars. My mother listened to the detailed bulletin he relayed to us with one of her almost invisible eyebrows raised. Pat had stopped wearing makeup and now had a face that was a clean slate, whatever went on behind it unwritten for anybody else to read. Her raised brow bone was as eloquent as if she'd stuck her tongue out and told us what she thought of her sister's latest brush with the Grim Reaper.

I assumed that nothing much went on in my mother's mind and that she had somehow unplugged it, so that the clatter of life going on around her was barely perceived background noise, elevator music. I thought the woman I remembered had burned herself out and had no joy left in her, and no memories, and certainly no traces of Miss Patricia Montgomery, St. Louis's bright star of the stage.

Pat outraged me, when I was a junior in high school, by proving just how wrong I was. A date picked me up to take me to a movie. He arrived half an hour early, and from my bedroom, as I hurtled into my clothes, I heard my mother's low voice, talking about how hot it was for April and what a suntan she was getting, just sitting out in our backyard.

She sounded social and relaxed. The boy guffawed at something she said. I snagged a stocking, tried to put my neck through the armhole of my dress and jerked the curlers out of my bangs. Frantic with anxiety, I made my entrance. My mother had pulled up her blouse and was showing my date her smooth brown back, with the white band of her bra bisecting it, while he looked on grinning foolishly.

I dragged him out of the house and jumped into his car before he could open the door. "Your mother's really something," he said when he came around to his side.

"You shut up," I said.

Though both would have been as shocked as I was, and would have let my mother the exhibitionist hear about it, I never told Roy or Ila Mae about this incident. I didn't warn them that the show girl was still in there, and that she still had a high kick left in her. I kept my own counsel, not because I was kind, but because I was thrown so badly off balance.

I had burst out, "Mother!" Pat looked at me with amusement and no apology at all. Lazily, she tucked her blouse in, said she hoped we had a nice time and trotted out her honeyed southern drawl to tell my escort, "Nice meeting y'all."

What made me want to kill her on that occasion, I know now, was that she had a powerful
sexual edge on me. An aged crone in her forties,
my mother could call up her former seductive self
effortlessly, a genie out of the bottle, and make her
nubile daughter vanish from sight, print summer
dress, Cuban-heeled shoes, Fire and Ice lipstick and
all. Worse, she thought this was funny.

Now that I am her age then, I remember this
scene with pride in Pat, and a whiff of middle-aged
envy. Her second marriage turned the living fireball into a cowed creature who no longer knocked
over bridge tables when belittled beyond tolerance,
and whose dancer's body had lost its taut-muscled
definition. Obeying the rhythm of her illness, she
checked in and out of Roy's life and mine like a
weary salesman checking into another cheap hotel,
indifferent to the decor and the company in the
dining room.

She could still transfix that teenaged boy with
the baring of her suntanned back and her husky
drawl, the low murmur that turned talk about the
weather into an intimate treatise on the pleasure
principle. As that unworthy audience for her female magic observed, when Pat chose to be she
was still really something.

THIRTEEN

~~~~~~

At eighteen, shortly after my freshman year in college, I got married. My mother and Roy gave me a steam iron. Ila Mae gave me two sets of sheets and pillowcases she had trimmed with embroidered borders, a lecture on sex along the lines of "We all have to do things we don't want to do sometimes" and two dozen blank thank-you note cards. Cy walked down the aisle as stiffly as if he were nailed to a board, after a sharp exchange between us in the anteroom of the Lutheran church in Missoula. I was wearing a white knit dress, a white satin pillbox hat and white satin pumps with three-inch heels. I loomed above Cy, who told me that I wobbled when I walked in those things and seemed to want me to take them off and make my journey to the altar stocking-footed. He must have thought I should make some concession since he couldn't wear his cowboy hat.

Roy boycotted the wedding. I had asked my father to give me away instead of asking him. He

wouldn't come at all, he said, because I had shamed
him so cruelly by this act of repudiation he couldn't
face people. Nor would he ever set foot again on
the same ground, hallowed or otherwise, with Cy.

Ila Mae and Wiley brought Pat, who took one
of her rare stands against Roy's authority by telling
him she would attend whether he came with her
or not. For the occasion, she resurrected a rose silk
dress that must have been twenty years old but still
had flair, even though it was tight for her and had
the only shoulder pads left in Montana. A neighbor gave her a home perm that turned her hair,
mostly gray by now, into tight corkscrews. She
made up her face and crammed her feet into ancient alligator pumps with open toes.

She looked very pretty, I told her as I pinned
on her gardenia corsage. My mother smiled with
great sweetness and apologized for her hands, holding them out for me to inspect. Her fingernails
were clipped short, and as they had been for many
years, were without nail polish. She said she had
wanted to "do" them but had no manicure tools
anymore. Did I know what had happened to the
set Cy gave her, in the red leather case?

I said it didn't matter and wondered when she had
last seen that manicure set. I also knew what had
happened to it. Anything Roy knew that Cy
had given either of us disappeared, sooner or later.
We had both learned early on not to ask what
had become of "junk" like missing manicure sets
or plastic statuettes of horses.

Pat and Dorothy met for the first time at that wedding. They introduced themselves to one another politely enough but could not conceal their mutual curiosity. Dorothy stared at my mother's thirties dress, the two round spots of rouge on her cheeks and her Little Orphan Annie permanent wave. My mother turned her good child's open gaze on Dorothy, in her mink stole and kelly green everything else.

Neither matched the other's image of her old rival for my father's love, a contest that never really existed other than in my stepmother's mind. Pat expected the auburn-haired nurse I had described so effusively as a child. Dorothy expected the face that had launched a thousand bronc riders. They looked at each other as if neither could believe her own eyes, two women thickening into middle age who had in common only that they had married the same man. When they weren't staring at each other, they stared at Cy, who was frozen with discomfort, as if searching for some clue to his inexplicable tastes.

Of the dearly beloved gathered together, only Ila Mae enjoyed that somewhat forlorn wedding, my leap into the idea of normalcy that prevailed at the time. Many of my high school friends were already married. Some of them had babies. Instead of pursuing acting careers, they were settling for what was possible, and greeted with warm approval in Missoula, and seemed smugly happy in their roles as young housewives. At her request, I had

given one of them a rolling pin as a shower present; she wanted a new kind that one filled with
ice water because it made flakier piecrust.

In the back of my mind, I knew mine was a
mismatch, and walked through the ceremony, head
held high, as if I were auditioning for a role I knew
I would not get. My father and my bridegroom, my
college drama professor, looked down upon each
other, neither of them impressed by the other's
credentials, and Cy played father of the bride with
bristling irritation. For Dorothy and Pat, the other
woman was the Ancient Mariner, though disap-
pointingly devoid of glittering eye. Instead, my
mother looked mildly out from beneath her hori-
zontal-comma eyebrows, drawn on with the old
painstaking care, and as it usually did, Dorothy's
mascara ran.

That left Ila Mae to rejoice in the ceremony,
which vindicated her formative role in my upbringing. I was being sensible, for once, instead of
following Pat into the world of greasepaint and
loose morals. I wouldn't be exposed to the rodeo
circuit anymore and so wouldn't relapse into
swearing when I wasn't showing off my vocabulary,
like Cy. Though he had earned back Ila Mae's good
opinion by becoming respectable, she still thought
plain speech was good enough for the Bible and
ought to be good enough for him.

Before my new husband and I drove away in a
shower of rice, my aunt passed on to me her accumulated domestic wisdom, standing on her toes
so that she could look me in the face or at least in

the chin. I was to remember who was the boss, never send shirts to the laundry, save the ends of bars of soap and press them together to make new bars, and when I no longer needed the diapers, hem them and use them for dish towels. I was not pregnant. Ila Mae was looking ahead.

My husband learned in her parting address to him that I was clean about my person, made my own clothes on my Singer sewing machine and could learn to cook if I put my mind to it. I had eaten good food at her table all those years, and so knew what it was. If my household management was so inept at first that he needed expert help, she was just a phone call away and would be there before he could say "too much starch in the collars." Into his jacket pocket, because I was carrying a nosegay rather than a purse, she tucked her recipe for icebox rolls.

Though it did not last long and caused as much pain as most failed marriages, mine freed me, finally, from my family. It removed me physically from my mother, whom I loved but whose custodianship Roy expected me to share, all the while pretending that Pat wasn't ill and needed no custodianship. By staying home from my wedding, and staging a noisy weeping scene behind his closed bedroom door while I was in my own room getting dressed in something old, something new and something borrowed (my bridegroom would slide on the blue garter, for the flash camera of the photographer), Roy hardened me against further emotional appeals he might make. He had a legitimate claim on me. It wasn't the claim he was making, one that precluded all other loyalties and that I had been resisting with more assertiveness as I got older.

He had raised me as Qualley. On my eighteenth birthday, I took back my legal name, Taillon.

As for Cy, my marriage elevated me, in my view, to parity with him. It proclaimed that I was an adult, who could do what I liked without his consent, and for whom another man was more important than he was. For the satisfaction I took in shooing my father off to the wings, for once, instead of being ushered into them myself, I was willing to master my aunt's icebox rolls and give up my career as the next Helen Hayes.

My husband and I moved to Oregon. Though none of us was in a league with Ila Mae, my mother, Cy and I kept in touch through letters. I rambled on cheerfully about married life, which wasn't cheerful in the least. My mother wrote about large events in her life, such as a new refrigerator. The refrigerator was the first major household purchase she and Roy had made since they'd set up housekeeping, in one afternoon, at Mr. Lucy's furniture store fifteen years earlier. Ila Mae's comment on this acquisition, when Pat wrote her about it too, was "too bad it had to be a Kelvinator."

Cy sent me twenty-five-dollar checks on birthdays and on the birth of my first child, and the unreadable last carbons of his schedules and his letters to the whole family. I had not seen him for two years when I made a last visit to him and Dorothy in Denver. Now that I regarded my father as an equal, I regarded Dorothy as an equal too and met her hostility head-on. Under the guise of girl talk, we sat in her spotless kitchen, over coffee, and skewered each other like chickens for the barbecue.

Dorothy told me how pretty I'd be if I ever learned to dress and if my skin ever cleared up. I told my overweight stepmother about the terrible metabolic curse I was under, how I stayed thin no matter how much I ate. I sighed and added that I guessed I was just like my father.

While we never tired of this sniping, and both perversely enjoyed it, Cy did, in a hurry. He turned his coldest green look upon me, one that could have frozen Lake Michigan in July, and got the same cold look back. It told him that his anger no longer turned me into a whimpering heap. Having no way of knowing that a nervous tic pulsed in my eyelid, he tried impressing his daughter into the deference due him.

At dinner one night, when there were guests present, he brought a bottle of Chianti to the table with a white napkin draped over his arm, ceremoniously pulled the cork and announced that he would pour it after it had time to breathe. I suggested maybe he should keep an oxygen tank around, in case the wine didn't start breathing on its own.

He itemized how much everything in the house had cost and showed me Dorothy's Grand Baroque

sterling silver, "the most expensive pattern made."
I thanked him warmly once again for his most recent twenty-five-dollar birthday check.

He told me he now drove Cadillacs, rather than
Buicks, because he had "a certain image to maintain." I told him I thought Cadillacs were osten-
tatious and for a split second thought my father
was going to swing on me.

Similarly, Dorothy gained no admiration from
me through her own steady stream of self-praise, a
conversational style she may have picked up from
long intimacy with Cy. For modesty's sake, these
compliments were always attributed to others. The
man who laid the wall-to-wall carpet had urged
Dorothy to become a professional decorator; he had
never met anyone with her color sense. Someone
had stopped her on the street in San Francisco to
tell her how nice it was to see an elegantly turned-
out woman for a change.

Years later, also in San Francisco, my stepmother startled me and a nearby table of diners
with the most singular of these spontaneous tributes. Her gynecologist, she announced loudly, had
said to her, "Mrs. Taillon, you have the uterus of
a young girl."

My father and Dorothy were equally unim-
pressed with me, a young woman with intellectual
pretensions and a pugnacious set to the jaw. It
never occurred to Cy that I had his temperament,
as well as his bone structure. He and Pat had taught
me never to run or even walk away from a fight, a
rule of life still dear to writers of Western songs,

and neither had thought to mention that I need not go out looking for one.

What angered Cy most in me was what he knew was also true of himself: that he was stubborn, demanded unqualified love from others and found it hard to forget, impossible to forgive. What angered me most about Cy was his rigidity, his total lack of warmth. Put my arms around him, and I was hugging a telephone pole. We kept our distance after that visit because father and daughter knew we had the same inflated pride, as well as the same cheekbones, and what we saw when we looked at each other made us both flinch.

I had to ask Cy for two hundred dollars when I fled my bad marriage. This wasn't the hardest part of extricating myself from it, but it was far from the easiest. He sent the money promptly, suggested that I live with a cousin in San Francisco while I was getting on my feet financially and emotionally, and filled two single-spaced pages with "if you had listened to your older and wiser father in the first place . . ." That he was right this time made his pointing out the obvious almost unbearable.

Cy announced the Grand National Western Livestock Exposition, in the San Francisco Cow Palace, for thirty-one consecutive years. The Cow Palace is a cavernous building shaped like a giant Quonset hut on the southern margins of the city, the rodeo a prosperous one whose main sponsor, for years, has been Winston cigarettes. A jumping-horse competition gives the proceedings an overlay of proper English classiness. Banners and flags fill the huge hall, floats are lowered from the ceiling and at the Grand Opening ceremonies rodeo dignitaries come out at the full gallop on horses doubly weighted with the silver on their saddles, bridles and stirrups. The cowboys who walk or limp away from the various events as PRCA champions have won as much as eighty thousand dollars for the year, as well as glory.

The riders and ropers at the Cow Palace are the best. The buckle bunnies are the prettiest, in their pearly cowboy hats and sprayed-on Western shirts and pants. Their boots are meant for dancing the two-step, after the rodeo, rather than riding. Their pink mouths open to let out piercing shrieks of "Ride 'em, cowboy! Hang in there, baby!"

Behind the arena and the chute area, where the vendors sell beer and hot dogs, the livestock exhibitors scrub bulls the size of small buildings with brushes and soapy water, rub them down as carefully as if they were fragile Chippendale chairs and await the judges with the clipboards, who'll get down on their hands and knees and inspect their entries from every angle. They're looking for perfect conformation, and Prime-grade flesh on the heavy bones, but it's a fair guess that when one is inspecting the undercarriage of such an animal, it gets a few points for having a friendly attitude.

The massive Winston scoreboard prints out times and scores electronically. When the honor guard rides out with the flags of the United States and California, their black horses have sparkle dust on their rumps, and the audience that applauds is saluting superb horseflesh along with all else for which America stands. Hats over their hearts, the crowd stands erect and still for the playing of "The Star-Spangled Banner," watching a faceted, reflecting ball revolving in the ceiling. It's the same lighting effect, but not the same crowd, one would find in a disco.

My father loved the Cow Palace rodeo, commanding the lavish spectacle and filling the enormous space with his voice from an announcer's stand almost lost in the vastness.

He liked descending on the big city in his latest Cadillac and taking up residence in his hotel just off Union Square. If people on the street did a double take at the sight of the small man in the Western suit, high-heeled boots, big hat and diamond horseshoe stickpin, they were simply struck by his fine clothes and good looks. He paraded furstoled and hatted Dorothy on his arm, fragrant in a cloud of perfume, as if the two of them owned the San Francisco sidewalks, and no doubt wondered why I hung behind, studying department store windows.

The Cow Palace board of directors included some of the city's prominent citizens, fine men Cy was proud to call his friends. The proprietors of his favorite restaurants recognized him from year to year, as they could hardly have failed to do, and Cy gave them both his patronage and tickets to the rodeo, expensive box seats he produced with a flourish. I also got free tickets, and one year shared a box with two Chinese cooks from Johnny Kan's and an Italian waiter from Fior D'Italia.

That was the year Cy deposited me in a downtown beauty salon to have my hair done before I appeared out at the Cow Palace. As I shook hands with the members of the board of directors, big, hearty men, I was miserable with self-consciousness under my bouffant, which looked as if it should have swallows nesting in it.

San Francisco was the high point of the circuit for Dorothy too. It was sophisticated, and unlike Chicago or Dallas, did not reek of the stockyards. Most of all, she liked the sidewalk flower stands, where my father bought violets for her furs. The city to which I had moved nonetheless alarmed them. Even before the hippies came along in their madras bedspreads of many colors, it had a reputation for both hedonism and excessive liberalism. It was full of interracial couples and homosexuals. I was involved with a man who was thirty-two years old and had never been married.

The dress code Dorothy remembered fondly, from years ago, no longer existed. Hatted and befurred women were the exception, not the rule, and Dorothy sighed for San Francisco's lost elegance.

The shape of my life further alarmed them. I picked them up one night in my male friend's old Volkswagen; veteran of so many spray-paint jobs, ranging from beige to army green, it was now mottled like army camouflage. I lived in a neighborhood not in the guidebooks, in an apartment above a grocery store reached by three flights of odorous stairs. I had joined a "Communist front organization," the ACLU. Cy was deeply relieved when he determined that I still used my married name.

I was too busy supporting myself and a child to be looking for fights anymore, especially not with my father. We fought constantly anyway, over whether the city I had embraced was or was not a cesspool. We fought over the man I would later marry, who never bought clothes and always needed a haircut.

"Your father's a short man," he said to me as we drove home from the rodeo one night. "You always talk about him as if he were a six-footer."

"Not short, *medium* height," I said. I thought I was abnormally tall, a giantess, and that this explained why I could look down on the top of Cy's hat.

I separated the man and the Western myth long enough to quarrel with Cy definitively, with such lingering wounds we did not see each other, and wrote no letters, for nearly eight years. In the early sixties, he and Dorothy came to San Francisco for the Cow Palace engagement as usual. They called me a day before they were about to leave. I rushed from the office where I worked to pay the short court visit that was all time allowed.

In the course of it, Dorothy suggested that I should put my young child up for adoption—I'd have a better chance of making an advantageous marriage. Considering the way I lived, in what amounted to a tenement, it was the kindest sacrifice a mother could make.

Did he agree with this advice? I asked Cy, who was roaming the room, gathering up notes and getting ready for the evening performance. We locked eyes for a long time. Of course he did, Cy said finally.

I walked out of his hotel room, determined never to see him again. And for years, when the rodeo was in town, I told my second husband that I was going to a movie and drove out to listen to my father's baritone voice rolling out in the darkness of the Cow Palace, setting off seismographs.

What a cornball the man is, I thought, what an insufferable strutting rooster, what a showboat. Then I'd think, you've got to hand it to him, though, he can sure as hell work a crowd.

FOURTEEN

~~~~~~

Until Cy's offer to let me apologize arrived, after all those years of silence on both sides, my only contact with the immediate family was with Dorothy. Shortly after I marched out of that San Francisco hotel room, she wrote me a letter she must have been composing as long as we had known each other. Its expressed intention was to make a better woman of me.

Again, she charged me with being an unfit mother, one who lived in an unfit apartment. She complained about the large sums of money Cy had given me, pointing out that when I lived with them in Oakland, she "went without to see you had decent clothes to go to school." The neon-green sweater and plaid skirt haunted her as much as they haunted me.

Most recently, they had invited me to Denver, where my time "was spent mostly in the company of that professor from Boulder. Who had quite a reputation as we bothered to find out."

Cy made no child support payments after the first years of his legal obligation, and few of them then. The professor was a seventy-year-old expert on George Bernard Shaw, with whom I'd had dinner once during my stay. If he had vices other than compulsive reading—bizarre sexual practices or heroin, say—he chose not to share them with me.

Dorothy's indictment ran on for two pages, unanswerable because her anger was irrational and bottomless. My former husband had not beaten me, she wrote. I must have divorced him because he did not make enough money "to give you the life you wanted." I had left my marriage because I was miserable in it, the reason most people leave marriages. My Catholic stepmother seemed to think the only grounds for divorce were compound fractures.

I knew Cy had read this outburst because Dorothy made no move without consulting him, not even planning the dinner menu. He added no postscript reading: "Disregard the foregoing." From that point on, Dorothy's resentment sat in the road leading to reconciliation between us like a heavily armored tank. I think we had equal respect for its fighting capabilities.

For Cy, Terry and Tommy, my stepmother's love was inexhaustible as the life force. By serving as my father's handmaiden, as well as his wife, she made Cy possible; her faith in him and her devotion to his career allowed him to become the man he became.

For her sons, she would have swum oceans or

got between them and a hand grenade. Their joys were Dorothy's joys, their setbacks her heavy blows, felt more profoundly than her children felt them.

But I was another woman's child, Cy's role in my existence irrelevant. He had "his own children" to consider, Dorothy told me once, when I asked him for a loan. It was a small loan. I needed it badly. Instead I got a forthright spelling-out that there was no room in my stepmother for what was not hers. Any defection from this view of things, on my father's part, would be seen as betrayal, parceling out his affections rather than delivering them whole.

What prompted Cy to write to me anyway, after nearly a decade, was learning that he had cancer. "This CA thing," as he called it, frightened my father and set him conducting a retrospective on his life, including the part of it he had banished from his résumé. From me, as well as from my brothers and Dorothy, he needed comfort, and moral support, and affirmation of his worth. The worst of his medical problems had been occasional laryngitis. Now he had cancer of the prostate; was ordered to quit smoking after forty years; had to endure treatments that he found painful and humiliating.

Other signs of physical failure assailed him, the loss of sight in his right eye for a few days and what sounds, in his highly circumspect description of it, like a stroke. He rolled a sheet of his letterhead into his portable typewriter and sent me a stiff-necked but unmistakable appeal for help, in toughing out the rest of his life and in mending his broken fences.

I wanted them mended as much as he did, though there was one section I was unwilling to prop up. "Life is too short to go on nursing old grievances," my father wrote me, meaning my grievances against Dorothy. "My own version of 'life is too short,'" I wrote back, "is that it's too short to keep beating one's head against the same stone wall." I could not forgive my stepmother her mean-spiritedness any more than Cy could forgive me for what he perceived as not loving him enough.

To his wife and sons, and to his fans, he had no flaws. To me, he had the usual number. Shaken by his illness, my father began to entertain the notion that while this was extremely unlikely, it was possible.

For the first time since I was a child, he wrote me personal letters instead of sending me carbons, telling me about money worries and disappointments. A rodeo he'd worked for thirty years had not renewed his contract for the following season. "Some of the younger announcers have greatly exaggerated my condition, and taken advantage of it."

Terry was wounded in Vietnam. Tommy was badly hurt in a bull-riding accident. My brothers made impulsive young marriages, as I had, and both were divorced. Cy told me how much anguish these events caused him, both on paper and on the phone, his voice querulous with complaint. "Cyra, old age is hell," he blurted in one conversation. My father was then in his early sixties.

Equally startling to me, because it was uncharacteristic, was his speculation in a letter that "perhaps I am now being punished for things I have done in the past." I replied that cancer was as arbitrary as a roll of the dice and that if there was a God, he hired no goons and kneecapped no one for being fallible. "Your ability to write is certainly reflected in your last long letter of November 2nd," Cy told me, moved by my mixed metaphors. I could recall no previous compliment from him, ever, and joked to my husband about hiring a stone carver.

Slowly, my father and I undertook the task of getting to know each other again, the most important in a long history of such efforts. Because I had not been around to see the process under way, I found it hard to grasp that Cy was as old as he was. My image of him was frozen in his early fifties, when I had last seen him, and even then I had not seen him realistically. Superimposed, always, on Cy in the flesh was the image of himself he'd invented and lived, the dashing cowboy celebrity. I had not seen him on the screen, doubling for Robert Taylor. One more ticket buyer, I had sat in the uppermost reaches of the Cow Palace, watching and listening to Cy a quarter mile away in the announcer's booth. On such occasions, the man for whom I was named was as unreal as an actor in a Western movie, and as inaccessible.

Nor had he any sense of me, living in the suburbs, remarried for ten years, going to school as a "re-entry woman." He did not know if there were "any little McFaddens," misspelled my daughter's name and could not remember how old she was, and politely asked after friends I had not seen since I was seventeen years old. Did I still keep up with my music? he inquired. I had no music to keep up with, as Cy damned well knew; listening to me attempt the national anthem with the rest of the crowd at rodeo openings, he'd shaken his head often enough and told anyone around it was a shame I was tone deaf.

I worked as a secretary for the San Francisco Opera for a few years, and must have told him about it. My job description underwent a transformation when he got hold of it and came back to me later, from someone he knew, as "I hear you sing with the opera company out there in San Francisco." "No," I said, and then, furious with Cy, added, "that was my mother."

It would have bewildered my father, with his P. T. Barnum approach to press agentry, that I did not appreciate his promotional efforts on my behalf. In wanting him to recognize that mine was a reasonable sort of life as it actually was, I was expecting a sculptor to put down his chisel and leave a block of marble intact. For Cy, the showman, one started with fact and took it from there, as far as invention would go.

A crowd at a rodeo was never a few hundred shivering souls, it was a thousand people cheering their lungs out. The hotel and dance-hall bands he had led, in his pre-rodeo days, became the Benny Goodman band and Cy the xylophone soloist. The radio program that featured my mother, in St. Louis, was the most popular program in the country and Pat competition for Sophie Tucker.

I was used to this facet of my father's character, and amused by it, but when it extended to me, I felt compromised. I was in my thirties, with children of my own, and Cy still hadn't acknowledged that he was stuck with the person I was, who would go to my grave with the same straight hair, would never be named Miss Rodeo America and was unlikely to shrink much.

Our letters were affectionate, when they began to travel back and forth every month or so. Cy congratulated me when I got my bachelor's degree. I congratulated him when he got favorable medical reports. Neither of us suggested meeting. We knew that we had best conduct our new accord at a distance, one at which we could sustain it. Had we risked getting together, other than on paper, we would have debated the shape of the conference table, my stepmother's motives and which station to listen to on the car radio.

Parents generally try to dominate their children. Children struggle to break free of them. My father's and my variation on this theme was that neither of us would yield a millimeter of ground, ever. Civilized in our relations with other people, we squared off at each other like a pair of pit bulls.

After twenty-five years of avoiding the mention

of her name, Cy asked about Pat. He wanted to know about the state of her health, and whether she was any happier these days, and confessed to an uneasy conscience about her. "In retrospect, I cannot help but believe that much of the difficulty between your mother and me was my own fault—much of it resulting from my immoderate drinking." As if this admission were disloyal, he followed with a paragraph about what good care Dorothy took of the house and of him, despite "a problem involving the nerve endings." Either he was being circumspect again or the problem had not yet been named to them. My father's much-loved wife and my old nemesis was in the early stages of Lou Gehrig's disease.

At a twelve-hundred-mile remove from them all, I began to realize, through their letters and calls, that my parents' lives, my stepparents' lives, Aunt Ila Mae's and Wiley's, were winding down, trailing off into an accumulation of illnesses and disappointments. Like Cy, all seemed to feel obscurely betrayed, only Pat incapable of surprise.

She wrote of breaking her leg in a sand trap while playing golf. Roy had taught her the game, the one form of recreation they shared. Fearful of telling him that she had been so clumsy, after she fell she played on until the leg was swollen and painful.

Pat's account of this accident is almost jaunty; it restored a little drama to her life. "I have to wear a cast!" she says, sounding pleased, and then pulls herself up short and adds a rote, Ila Mae–like pietism: "However, with God's help I will golf again."

From Roy, not long afterward, I heard of a more serious event in her life, a radical mastectomy. I'd fly home, I told him. Roy was mysterious about the reasons, on his end of the phone, but made it plain that he did not want me there. The house was too small. The trip would be a waste of good money. In the summer, he said, he'd bring my mother to California to visit my family instead.

Although I could have pointed out that I'd been home many times before, and the house had held us all then, I didn't argue. For years Pat had not been more than a few miles from the block on which they lived. Such a journey, for her, would be on a scale with Lindbergh's in "The Spirit of St. Louis." My less altruistic motive was that I hated the Missoula bungalow, with its storm windows in place the year round, so that the air inside was stale and oppressive, and its peculiar smell of vitamin capsules and the sprouted wheat Roy grew in the bathtub.

His health-food preoccupation had become a passion. We started the mornings there with the viscous brew he whipped up for breakfast in his indispensable blender, blackstrap molasses and twenty-one other ingredients outside any normal definition of food. By now, my stepfather's theory was that if it tasted good, it was trying to kill you. Behind his back, Pat and I made terrible faces over our khaki-colored health shakes. Roy left for the candy company. We poured them down the toilet in the bathroom, making our way around the amber waves of grain.

The Ila Mae Chronicles escalated my mother's loss of a breast to both breasts and stated darkly that her doctors weren't telling her the whole truth. "Once It get started it go right thru you, they can cut It out but It pop out somewhere else, Susie her Days Are Numbered. I can't do anything for her only Pray, that I do for the whole world."

She moved on to world affairs:

> Our town is full of Rape stabbings and dope. Last night 12 year old girl was stabbed six times in her home. He tried to Rape her. Didn't make it, he was just out of prison. Few weeks ago 9 year old girl was Raped all most died they haven't caught the man yet. The police said no woman should be out after dark.
>
> So have good day for I love you all.

The blow dealt Wiley worried me more than the latest crime wave in Great Falls. For thirty years, he worked for the same downtown department store, selling suits, ties and what he considered the height of elegance for men, white-on-white shirts. The store was a genteel anachronism, with a cafeteria in the basement that offered weary shoppers chicken salad and angel food cake, and a staff of Wiley-like employees, old family retainers who'd spent their adult lives behind its counters writing up sales of Ladies Necessaries and Better Chocolates.

In the seventies, the store was sold to a large chain. The chain fired Wiley a few weeks before he would have been entitled to retirement benefits. He got a job at J. C. Penney's after a few anxious months, but at Penney's he was no longer "our Mr. Gosney." Ila Mae wrote that he had developed a bleeding ulcer and that the piped-in music in the menswear department made his ears ring.

My mother and father had been adventurers, performers who wrote their own scripts, starring themselves, and expected even the people they loved best to function as the supporting cast. Dorothy played her own fulfilling role as wife of the great man. Wiley plodded along, not thinking very deeply about where a day led. Ila Mae saw the world through her kitchen window but took her limited raw material and wrote it large, interpreting life for the rest of us in its rich, rape-and-murder-ridden variety. Roy made a vocation of injured merit. Now, with the exception of Pat, who accepted broken legs, mastectomies and wheat in the bathtub with the same passivity, they all seemed to feel they were the victims of injustice, in the form of mortality.

At Christmas, Roy sent me a gift subscription to *Prevention*, a magazine that reflected his views about diet and health maintenance. "Your health is all you have got," his card read. Pat's motto had been "Your looks are all you've got." Ila Mae lived for Judgment Day, when God would reward the good and punish the sinners. My father wanted above all to be Somebody. With the end of his rodeo days in sight, he felt the way he must have felt without his cowboy boots on, insubstantial and reduced to ordinariness.

Through their letters ran a strain of melancholy: where had their lives gone? Even Ila Mae, awaiting vindication beyond earthly glory, had doubts about her belief system. God would pin a good conduct medal on her for the suffering she'd endured, she knew, but he was unaccountably taking His own sweet time about it.

FIFTEEN

Wiley was the first to die. He left the world without a fuss after an illness of a week, a workhorse dropping in his traces. My aunt mourned him so deeply we all worried about her. Their marriage, to outsiders, resembled a Punch-and-Judy show. Mysteriously, it was a close marriage all the same, Ila Mae's nagging and Wiley's automatic "Aaa, shut up" their own form of intimate communication.

Cy was on the road when Wiley was buried, but he called on Ila Mae when he was back in Great Falls, the first visit he had paid in years. Time was tearing down barriers between my father and the people he cared about when he was young, or who cared about him; he was seeing his life whole now, rather than in installments. Coming full cycle, he and Dorothy had sold the Denver house and moved back to Great Falls, a few blocks from the house in which Dorothy grew up.

Roy was next. The oldest, he was also the sturdiest, because of his health regimes or in spite of them, and at seventy-eight was still working part-time at the candy company. No longer on the payroll, he helped out at inventory time, in the warehouse, and spent the day he died shifting packing cases. Neighbors called me late the following night to tell me about his death. My mother, they said, had just remembered she had a daughter in California.

At the airport in Missoula, where they drove her out to meet my plane, Pat waited behind the barrier, wearing a cheap platinum-blond wig, slightly askew, and her sweet, vague smile. "Why, hello, dear," she said, surprised. If she knew why I was there, the information was tucked somewhere back in the reaches of her mind. Behind her, the husband of the neighbor couple tapped the side of his head significantly and rolled his eyes

My stepfather died of a sudden heart attack. Pat called 911, rehearsed by him in how to pick up the receiver and dial the three numbers, but he was dead when the ambulance arrived a few moments later. She told the story while I helped her get ready for bed, anxious about getting the details right but dry-eyed. Roy seemed to be vanishing from her memory as quickly and painlessly as he had died in his easy chair, still wearing his hat and overcoat. In his musty room, with its lonely double bed, I lay awake chain-smoking and thought how quickly the house would burn if I were careless. The rugs were thick with dust, the windows hermetically sealed and hung with moldering curtains, the room strung with a maze of frayed electrical cords. Health-food books, piled up on the bureau, on Pat's long-unused vanity table and along the walls, made the passage to the bed a narrow tunnel. I knew why Roy had fended off visitors.

The man who'd had the terrible nightmares in that room lay in a local funeral home, which had left several urgent telephone messages. The gist of these was that the deceased aren't good keepers. I knew Roy wanted his body flown home to Wisconsin, because Pat had come out of her stupor long enough to tell me so, and I got out of bed to look for his address book. For most of the night I went through drawers stuffed full of paper, finding only old order pads, yellowing junk mail and on a closet shelf a paper bag crisscrossed with Scotch tape. On it, Roy had written: "LAETRILE. *Illegal*. Pat, do not tell anyone, in the event of my death, destroy." The contents looked like fine brown dust.

My stepfather and mother, Ila Mae and Wiley had come to see me and my family two summers ago, as Roy had promised. They made a slow trip in the Dodge Dart Roy bought when the station wagon began to send up clouds of smoke, stuck close to my suburban house for a week and then set off for home and safe haven again. I made them promise not to continue a practice that terrified me when I rode with them on their lone excursion into San Francisco, stopping in the middle of the freeway to look around. Cars skidded and blared around them. Roy studied the map unhurriedly and honked back at them.

The Dart had less than a thousand miles on it. Like Roy's bedroom, it smelled musty, and it started hard because it was driven so little. Stalling at every intersection, it made my mother and me late for Roy's funeral two days after I arrived.

In the interest of saving money, I had picked out the cheapest coffin in the funeral home. I regretted it when I saw my stepfather laid out in what looked like a Styrofoam picnic chest. The undertaker had rouged Roy's cheeks and made his mouth rosy with lipstick. I felt an acute pang of sympathy for him, looking androgynous, and mortified about it, beneath his layer of makeup.

Another pang seized me when the few mourners arrived, members of Roy's Masonic lodge alerted by the notice in the newspaper. The lodge brothers did not know him. The older he grew, the more reclusive Roy became, imprisoning himself and Pat in the airless house, venturing out to buy more lecithin capsules and the sacks of worm-infested grains that filled the kitchen cupboards. Equipped with his blender and a few pots and pans, he had taken over the cooking. At the all-you-can-eat smorgasbord where I took Pat for our meals, I watched her pile her tray with plates of cream pie.

Although she cried at the funeral, her tears were perfunctory, as if she sensed that tears were expected of her. She and I were to fly Roy's casket home, to be buried in the family plot, the following day. That night I began clearing out the refrigerator, empty except for the ranks of brown bottles full of vitamin capsules. Pat was asleep. I worked quietly so that she would not see me performing this task and be upset by it.

My mother appeared in the kitchen doorway, in her nightgown. She saw the trash bag at my feet and reached into the open refrigerator, picked up a bottle and slammed it into the bag, with the speed and coordination of a major-league pitcher. Before she went back to bed, she joined me in a beer and a cigarette. I spent a macabre morning filling out shipping orders for Roy's remains, referred to by the airline personnel as Mr. Qualley and "it." Pat sat in the waiting room, her suitcase at her feet, restless with anticipation. On the plane, she sat pressed to the window, looking out into the cloud banks, until the stewardess brought lunch. "This is on me," she told me graciously. "I insist." In Roy's sister's house in Oconto, over and over, she told the assembled family about the manner of Roy's death.

"He said to me, 'Dear, I'm tired. I think I just want to sit here and rest.' Then he said, 'Sweetheart, I've got a bad pain in my chest, call the ambulance.' " Each time Pat told the story, enjoying being the focus of attention, she incorporated more endearments into it, loving pet names Roy had never spoken. She was describing their marriage, for posterity, not as it was but as she wanted it to be. In the coquettish blond wig, from which she refused to be parted, she put on a last performance, transforming life into art.

The Wisconsin relatives, kind people who liked "Patty," listened and nodded and wept with her.

I went into my Aunt Babe's kitchen and drank with Uncle Norman, Roy's oldest brother.

Norman preferred bourbon to the hot dishes and sheet cakes neighbors brought to the front door all that week. In the pocket of his plaid wool jacket, food-stained and tobacco-smelling, he had a pint flask, from which he poured an inch into a cheese glass for me. In silent complicity, we bolted the bourbon down, then stood leaning against the counter. "Poor old son of a bitch," Norman said gravely. He had pronounced his brother's most eloquent eulogy.

A young Lutheran minister delivered the more formal eulogy at the graveyard, where I was shamed again by my taste in coffins. In late October, in Wisconsin, snow lay on the ground. A gray sky sent down a drizzle, and Aunt Babe passed around umbrellas to the dozen of us present. Pat cried once more, tears that stopped almost as soon as they started, but seemed more bewildered than grieving. Among her clothes, I'd had trouble finding a dark dress that fit her and a warm coat. The garments I had finally packed were so old they gave her that look, again, of a woman in a period movie.

Now that the week of sorting out Roy's affairs was behind me, it struck me with full force that my mother was helpless, a woman who had not driven a car for twenty years, could not write a check and responded to my "It's Cyra, Mother" on the phone with a thoughtful pause followed by "Who?" Back in Missoula, I began the paperwork for putting her house on the market and found a convalescent home for her.

The day I took her there, my stomach churned with guilt. I was the parent now, and she was the child, and I was abandoning her.

Pat bounced on her bed, testing the mattress, put her clothes in the bureau and the closet, and in a cracked mirror applied lipstick to her mouth with her little finger, peering closely at her reflection. She was in some small town in the Midwest, forty years ago, getting ready to play the provinces.

After the long, stifling captivity of her marriage, my mother found the convalescent home stimulating and wrote me cheerful letters about small events in her day. To make the letter writing easier, I sent her stamped envelopes with printed return-address stickers on them. She crossed out "Mrs. Roy Qualley" above her address and painstakingly lettered in "Patricia."

Cy asked me to convey his sympathy, when I told him about her new circumstances, and wrote that he would contact her "at the first opportunity." That he never did had nothing to do with insincerity but with his wariness of the past, and the pain that confronting it held for him. Everyone who knew the ruinous rakehell in the old photographs had forgiven him except for Cy himself.

"Don't come to see him Susie," Ila Mae wrote. "You wouldn't recognize him & he wouldn't want you to see him This way." Cy was a walking skeleton. Dorothy wasn't much better. "She have some terrible disease, some famous baseball player got it. It incurable." Terrible diseases being no excuse for letting oneself go, she noted that Dorothy had gained more weight. "Also, she *huge*."

My aunt sounded the death knell for Cy prematurely. Though he pared down his schedule to a dozen rodeos a year, he kept on working, telling people that he was retiring and would spend his time writing and trout fishing. In 1977, taking note that he was not appearing at the Cow Palace as usual, a writer for the San Francisco *Examiner* referred to him as "slick Cy Taillon . . . a legend who looked like Spade Cooley and sounded like the Reverend Billy Graham."

In Lewiston, Idaho, a reporter wrote of "a voice that rose and fell with each passing crisis on the arena floor below, investing even the prosaic with an element of excitement." By then Cy had announced the Lewiston Roundup for twenty-nine years.

Thirty-one years at the National Western in Denver. Thirty-eight at the Western Washington State Fair, where, for a decade, photographed as a six-year-old in cowgirl regalia, I had been a poster girl. These rodeos were constants in my father's life, and he kept presiding over them despite depression, trouble breathing and "the increasing pain and distress . . . of this cancer thing." Part of the Western ethic was that cowboys die with their boots on. Reading me the latest tribute over the phone, marking his farewell appearance one place or another, he told me irritably, "They're lining up behind the bone wagon, and I'm not even dead yet."

In 1979, a package arrived from him. He was going through memorabilia and thought I might like to have my baby pictures.

I knew that if I didn't see my father soon, I wouldn't see him alive again. I stayed home in California. By the time Cy was hospitalized for what was to be the last time, in 1980, my husband had borne out my theory of the randomness of the lightning bolt. He also had terminal cancer.

Don't come, Terry said on the phone when I made a halfhearted offer. Remember him the way he was. My brothers and I had not seen each other for ten years either, but out of empathy for me, as we watched the people we loved best dying, Terry let me off one more emotional hook. So did Cy. "It wouldn't do me any good," he said the last time we talked on the phone, and seeing him could only cause me pain. At least, he assumed it would cause me pain.

"You know it would," I snapped.

"Well, I certainly hope so," my father snapped back. For us, this exchange was an unprecedented admission of love.

My brother Terry has a growly, good-old-boy Western voice. "We lost him," it told me when he called in mid-April of 1980. Agonizing as it was to see him go, he went on, it was a mercy. Cy had been in terrible pain for days, and so heavily

drugged he wasn't anyone we both knew. "Cyra,"
Terry said through tears, "he was as spaced out as
a soup sandwich."

I said I'd lost Cy a long time ago. My brother
took exception. "He always loved you."

I wanted to believe this. I also wanted the impossible: to live my life over again, with Cy remaining present in it, not as the parent I could not
please but as the father I remembered from my
childhood, dangerous but dashing, who'd taught
me the words to "San Antonio Rose." Into my
scrapbook, Cy Taillon's daughter in spite of him
and myself, I pasted the newspaper editorials that
people I barely knew sent me from all over the
West.

Dorothy followed Cy a few months later, and in
some unfathomable scheme of things, it was her
deathbed that found me in attendance. Pat had
suffered a series of strokes. I went to Missoula to
move her into a nursing home. Before I turned
around and went back to California, I drove to
Great Falls to see my brothers, as adults. With my
family "passing away," in the gentle euphemism,
one after another, I felt the need to hang on to
the relatives I had left.

I stayed at the Cosgriff house with Dorothy's
sisters, in the bedroom I used to stay in all those
lifetimes ago. We went out to dinner at the same
steak house across the Misssouri River where we
all used to go when Cy was in town, and where
he'd once exasperated me by sending a bottle of
wine back. He claimed it was "off."

As is usually the case in Montana, the wine was chilled just short of being frozen solid. Alexis Lichine couldn't have pronounced on its merits or said, for sure, whether it was red or white. Cy still got a stricken apology from the waiter, who brought him another bottle, or possibly the same one, bowing from the waist.

"Much better," my father said regally, without tasting it.

Dorothy was in a nursing home too. She had asked urgently that I come to see her, her sisters said. I went, reluctant but deeply curious; what did she want from me, near the end of her life, and what could we find to say to each other? The nursing home turned out to be the hospital in which I was born, fallen on hard times. My stepmother had done her nurse's training there, under the watchful eye of the nuns. It was hard to imagine the young, auburn-haired Dorothy, in her starched white cap, as the same woman who lay in bed, almost immobilized, no longer my antagonist or anyone's.

Her eyes were as extraordinary as I remembered, large and brilliant, with the familiar wistful expression. They locked on me as I stood beside her and listened to her tell me about her marriage to my father, "the greatest love story ever told." Their ashes would be mingled, she said, so that the two of them would be together in death as they were in life.

While she spoke, I looked at the picture of Cy on the wall of her room, an enormous blowup of a black-and-white photo. In it, he accepted one more award, a plaque or a silver and gold belt buckle, a compellingly handsome man in a Western suit and cowboy hat photographed from somewhere down around his knees, so that he looked tall as a tree.

He not only loomed above me, he loomed above Dorothy. Of all the people who had loved him and lived in the shadow he cast, I thought, only my stepmother had never felt diminished or chilled by it. With an exhausting effort of will, she was serving the legend still, testifying to her part in it to me, the only unexplained interruption of the tale of the schoolgirl and the piano player. I needn't have worried about what to say. I had been summoned there to listen.

SIXTEEN

Cy said that Bennett Cerf urged him to write his autobiography; his was a singularly colorful American life. I began my version the year before he died, intending it to be a journalistic account of his career. The book refused to remain the one I set out to write, the one Cy himself might have written. It wasn't Cy Taillon the celebrity that I needed to make sense of but my onetime polestar, and Roy's obsession, and the hell-for-leather cowboy my mother had sung about loving come rain or shine.

Two years after our father's death, I asked Terry to take me to Miles City, where he had announced his last rodeo. Cy's ghost would be there. I thought it would be pleased to know his adult children, strangers for so long, had reclaimed each other as family, and that I was in the process of reclaiming him.

My brother and I traveled the same route that Cy took out of Great Falls, across eastern Montana and vast expanses of sagebrush, sand cliffs and emptiness. The landscape is dun-colored except for white spots on the horizon, the tails of grazing antelope. Alongside streams, cabins with no roofs stand abandoned, swallows their tenants. The cold winters, or the loneliness, proved too much for the homesteaders who built them. Said Terry, pointing to one of them, "Somebody's dream . . ."

With years as a bronc rider and a rodeo judge behind him, Terry had begun announcing. He was not appearing at Miles City. Though he is following in Cy's bootsteps, he is reluctant to step in them. "Those boots left holes too big for me to put my feet in."

The Western songs he played on his tape deck were the old songs. The bars we stopped at were the same bars, timeless, preserved in their amber light. When we pulled into Miles City on Friday night, the town was unchanged to my eyes although I had not been there for twenty-five years. The false-front one-story buildings on Main Street still looked like the set for a Western movie. Had I leaned against one of them, I would have expected to plunge through a plywood façade. The sale started on Saturday, but Miles City was already full of horse trailers and pickup trucks, the Olive Hotel bar full of stock contractors.

Solidly muscled men, nicknamed Red and Scrapiron, the contractors "signify" because they have earned respect on the backs of broncs or in brawls, the kind Miles City talks about the way veterans talk about the Normandy landing. Shoulder to

shoulder in the bar, with its low-lying pall of cigarette smoke, they traded jokes and set up drinks
for each other and for us.

Though the Bucking Horse Sale is a relatively
small rodeo, it is famous in the West because producers come there to bid on the horses that may
make them rich. Cy announced it one last time,
on a rainy weekend, when he was easily exhausted
and in pain. If it's not hot in Miles City in May,
it's so cold that after a few hours at the fairgrounds
on the outskirts of town, slogging through icy mud,
you keep looking down, making sure your feet have
not been amputated. The cold must have pene-
trated Cy's bones.

The traditional Friday-night itinerary is to go
from one of the bars that line Main Street to the
next. The Bucking Horse Sale is a notoriously
rowdy event that turns Miles City inside out once
a year, to the collective civic pride of the place,
and alcohol fuels the good fellowship and the
fights. Until recently, the city aided and abetted
the drinking by closing off several blocks to truck
and car traffic, so that celebrants could go from one
bar to the other with drinks in hand. The sale was
a drunken orgy, local clergy and an out-of-state
newspaper complained, telling Miles City what it
already knew, and finally, the city sighed and
passed an open-container law. Now the contractors, the cowboys and the crowd that comes simply
to whoop and holler have to stand packed together
inside the bars and relay drinks over each other's
heads.

At the Bison, where Terry and I dug in for the evening, the passing of drinks resulted in frequent deluges down the backs of our necks. Conversation blurred into an amorphous roar. Somewhere in the back, a Western trio played to nobody in particular, the lot of musicians in bars the world over. Brusque and efficient, the bartenders wore Gay Nineties dress. They darted back and forth like water bugs while I knocked back whiskey ditches with Terry, calculating his body weight as opposed to mine and wondering if we'd eaten dinner that night. Approximately 960,000 people live in Montana. Most of them seemed to be in the Bison, pleased to see Terry and deaf to my pleas of "Oh no, thanks a lot, but really, I've had enough." His eyes hidden behind black sunglasses, Terry grinned down at me. One of my brother's favorite sayings is: "If you can't run with the dogs, don't piss with the puppies."

So I drank with him, and the rest of the crowd, and tried to catch the punch lines of the stories that all begin, a popular joke has it, "This ain't no bullshit . . ." The press of other bodies, and pride, kept me upright. Around midnight, beside me in the crush, a young cowboy tapped me on the shoulder. "I must be taken into consideration," he said.

Echoes of Willy Loman and "attention must be paid." "How come?" I asked.

"Because I lost my hat. Somebody done took it."

"You can get another one."

"I can't, neither. That was the Beethoven's Ninth of hats."

This exchange seemed hallucinatory, but so did being back in my father's world. I had walked away from it. There it was, tapping me on the shoulder and insisting on being taken into consideration. I knew that to Terry, and to the genial crowd at this bar, Cy had epitomized the last line of defense in a country gone to the dogs, the liberals and Gloria Steinem.

The Western wives I remembered were present too, handsome women who sat a barstool as stylishly as they sat a horse and who told the same breathtakingly sexist and racist jokes their husbands told. "This is a good one, honey," they said, launching into them, friendly and welcoming. They reminded me that the West is still a male world, one in which women are admired for how well they imitate men. On the ranches, these women did the same hard work, taking the pickup out in blizzards to hay the horses; shearing the sheep on sheep ranches and putting up with the smell that permeates clothing with a foul lanolin reek; sharing the driving on the rodeo circuit, with the kids, the blue heeler dog and a horse trailer in tow. I decided not to lobby for the ERA that night.

These women enjoy the lives they have chosen, thank you, and if I saw them as patronized, they didn't. Nor did they mind the affectionate references to "the ball and chain here," perhaps because they knew that if they got fed up with his chippying around, they could bring their man back into the corral like any experienced pickup rider. Lecturing a Montana ranch wife about women's lot at the hands of the male oppressor is asking to get your face rearranged.

The Bison closed at three in the morning. Terry and I were propelled out into the street by a flying wedge of merrymakers behind us. We stood swaying on the sidewalk, confronted with a line of helmeted policemen fingering riot clubs.

Miles City brings in police from Billings to maintain order for the Bucking Horse Sale, a hopeless undertaking. In the afternoon, they had patrolled in pairs, checking out the bars and making themselves visible. By seven o'clock, they traveled in fours. At bar-closing time, they were deployed eight strong, figuring that their small margin of strength lay in numbers. The Billings police are deeply resented, by the rodeo crowd, as foreign mercenaries. For some atavistic reason, they were resented that night by me. "I hate those old boys," my brother said. His arm, draped over my shoulder, felt weighty as a redwood log. The two of us fixed the police between us and Terry's car in a hostile gaze.

"Hell," I heard myself saying. "They're not so big, let's take 'em." I had picked out my four, and Terry's, and this idea seemed entirely reasonable.

My brother wrestled me to the car and drove back to my motel. Before he said good night, he told me I was showing signs of turning into trouble.

Saturday morning, badly hung over, we drank

Bloody Marys and pushed around eggs in the motel coffee shop, where the breakfast special was twelve-ounce buffalo steaks. More friends of Terry's, and Cy's, stopped by our table to say hello. "Cy's daughter," they said to me. "Well, I'll be damned, where you been?" They were open, and sociable, and I still found them unnerving, these men whose gaze was skilled at appraising horseflesh.

By the time we got out to the fairgrounds, Miles City was running true to form for the Bucking Horse Sale weekend. The rain fell steadily, wetter than other rain, and in the arena, gumbo mud turned the rider who got bucked off his horse into a human Fudgsicle. Gumbo is slick and black, with enough suction to swallow a three-year-old child. You can't walk in it without using both hands to pull one foot clear, and then the other, and if you drive through it, it becomes part of your car. In a reaction to the rhinestone cowboy syndrome that brings out the Taillon in me, I had worn shoes to Miles City instead of boots. I own cowboy boots, but so do computer programmers, hairdressers, rock stars and buyers for Macy's. They belong on cowboys.

The result of this principled choice was that I sank into the freezing gumbo up to my ankles. It climbed my pants legs and oozed over my shoe tops. Said Terry, looking at my feet with compassion and scorn, "You forgot. Never go to a rodeo unless you don't care what you step in."

The only events at the rodeo were bareback and saddle-bronc riding, intended to show off the horses rather than the riders, some of whom were weekend cowboys and young kids from the surrounding ranches. Since 1951, the contractors who supply rodeo stock have come to the Miles City sale to buy bucking horses at auction. Immediately after each ride, the auctioneer starts the bidding. While sellers bring in horses from all over the West, many are local. A rancher finds he has a horse that bucks, a trait that cannot be bred into an animal and makes him useless as a working ranch horse. He brings him to Miles City and hopes he'll show what he's made of, thereby entering the ranks of the elite in the rodeo world. Highly prized, bucking horses have careers that outlast those of the cowboys who ride them and who get to know every horse on the circuit—their cranky personalities, their bone-shattering moves. As catered to as coloraturas, these horses become legends in their own right.

The sale published a Collector's Edition program that year, one with a moving tribute to Cy in it. It contained a lengthier tribute to a horse named Skyrocket. "There were many other great horses, like Limber Jim, Bovee Grey, Flying Devil and the Spinner, but Skyrocket captured the heart of Montana." Six men managed to ride him before he died, after twenty years of putting cowboys in full-body casts.

Terry explained the scoring to me as the first rider shot out of the chute, to be bucked off, hard, when the horse nearly lost its footing. Both rider and horse are judged; the scoring is 1–25 for the rider, 1–25 for the horse. There are two judges, for a total of 100 possible points.

The horses are judged on how high they buck and how powerfully. "Look for the extension of the back legs in the kick, and at the withers. That's where the power is in a bucking horse."

Riders are judged on how securely they sit, on how far forward they keep their feet and on their spur stroke. The rider should spur the horse from shoulder to rump with smooth strokes of blunted spurs, which agitate but don't hurt the horse. Though the spurs will sometimes draw blood on a thin-skinned thoroughbred, bucking-horse stock is too highly valued to be abused. Over the afternoon, at the end of the auctioneer's glossolalia, sales prices ranged from one hundred thirty to twelve hundred dollars, for a black horse that tried to dismantle the bleachers and the cowboy on his back. In previous years, horses have sold for as much as the compact cars most cowboys still wouldn't be caught dead in.

The metal grandstands were open to the weather. I had not brought enough warm clothes with me to Miles City, and the rain drilled through my city slicker. My head throbbed from the bourbon I had drunk the night before. My throat closed on the hot dogs I tried to put down it, the only fare at the concession stand besides beer. Amazed at how much, I missed Cy's voice over the p.a. system; the pilgrimage I had insisted upon struck me as a mistake, a trip back to a world in which I did not belong, and hadn't for most of a lifetime.

Beside me sat the brother I scarcely knew, his cowboy hat soaked through despite its plastic cover, immune to the cold. Terry worked the chutes when he wasn't dutifully keeping me company. He wished he were riding again, he told me, and I wanted to shake him; hadn't he broken enough bones yet? What he replied paraphrases loosely as "A man's gotta do what a man's gotta do."

Tommy, too, was waiting to turn forty so he could ride Brahma bulls in "old-timers" rodeo, held together though he was with steel pins and Superglue. Tending bar in Colorado once, my younger brother had been shot in a fight he was trying to break up. In Great Falls, before Terry and I left, I asked him for particulars. Tom said it was no big deal, the gunshot missed all of his vital organs and the helicopter that evacuated him to the nearest hospital got there right away.

Our father had spent his life promoting this chest-beating ethic. I realized that I'd found it more comprehensible as a child than I now found it as an adult, and as the rodeo and the rain continued, worked myself into a fouler and fouler mood.

Interspersed with the bareback and saddle-bronc riding at the Bucking Horse Sale are quarter-horse races. It was already dark, at midday, when the track announcer took over for the rodeo announcer, who, at the beginning of the day, had called for a moment of silence in memory of Cy Taillon.

The track announcer asked us to put money in a hat over at the beer stand, a collection for "a cowboy who planned to be here today but didn't make it. He was in a car crash, and had an ear tore off and other minor injuries." This appeal sank in slowly. When it did, the crowd burst into mighty guffaws.

"What do you suppose a major injury is?" my brother asked, laughing so hard himself that his eyes were watering. I didn't know, and couldn't have answered through my own laughter, but I didn't care: that only-at-a-rodeo announcement had replaced my feeling of strangeness with familiar affection, for Miles City, for the sport my father loved, and for Cy.

Even when he was close to dying, he would have been in his element here. He would have made us forget the cold, by stamping our feet and cheering the riders on; pulled out the organ stops until the hat at the beer stand overflowed with money; forgotten his own discomfort, and all else, as long as he had a microphone in his hand.

I thought, with no irony at all, that it wasn't cancer that had killed my father, it was being unplugged.

Terry, Cy and Tommy.

Roy, Ila Mae and Wiley.

Cyra's high school graduation photo, Class of '55.

Cyra.

A somber Cy in his early sixties.

Pat and Roy in
their late years.

Pat and Ila Mae in Lincoln, Montana,
in the early 1970's.

Terry, Cyra and Tommy together in 1982.

CODA

Here are some excerpts from the yellowing pages I carry around from one side of the country to the other, in old hatboxes that once belonged to Roy.

Ila Mae to Pat, sometime in the spring of 1982:

Dear Pat, It has been such long time since I have had any news from you you are all ways on my mind cause I love you . . . Please dear let me hear from you. Some one will read this for you Some one will write note for you. I worry about you . . .

Roy to me, undated:

I know you have to consume spirits at all the partys you attend and possibly more than is good for you. If such is the case, you should eat a lot of asparagus, that cleans out all the ammonia in your system. The least harmful of all liquors is vodka made from potatoes; and be sure you get a lot of B-vitamins in your diet. I hope you have a nice exmas and take care of your health. As ever.

Cy to me, 1975:

I must tell you how proud I am of you in your pursuit of an education and in the reaping of the fruits of your efforts now. The important thing now is for you to realize happiness in the short life span allotted to all of us . . .

Ila Mae to me, undated:

Well Dear Keep up the good work just remember that John comes First. This clipping was in our paper the Great Falls Tribune, isn't this terrible? . . .

Each time I move, I ask myself why I keep this accumulation of letters. The writers are all dead; throwing away their correspondence could offend none of their sensibilities. Yet I preserve all these thousands of words, Roy-like, as if they were encoded and someday I will crack the cipher, understand the nature of my family's affections and jealousies. I will learn to see them all through their own eyes, instead of imperfectly through mine.

Ila Mae tyrannized Baby Sister from their days in Paragould, chastising her for everything from marrying Cy, to leaving Roy, to crooked seams up the backs of her stockings. In the months before she died, she wrote Pat almost daily, telling her how much she loved her, and instead of newspaper photos of child polio victims, enclosed dime-store valentines. Their mottoes read: "You're sweet as honey" and "You're very special, be mine," and they are meant for small children.

Roy named me his heir, after my mother. The language of his will says he does so "because I look upon her as my own flesh and blood."

When we drew close again, at our cautious re-move, Cy wrote often about how proud he was of me for getting a book published. All the praise he had withheld for a lifetime, he heaped on me then, sending me interviews in which he mentioned me as "the other writer in the Taillon family." A sen-tence in his will excluded me. I wanted nothing from him, and expected nothing, but found it pain-ful to be struck once again from the rolls of his children. He had acknowledged my existence inter-mittently. It made me smile a peculiar smile that my copy of the will, mailed to me by a North Dakota law office, arrived with fourteen cents postage due.

My mother, the one who had the greatest ca-pacity to surprise, gave me the most unassimilable proof that I had not really known her. Soon after my husband died, I drove to Montana again to visit her. We sat on the porch of the nursing home, in a thin winter sun, and I told Pat that Ila Mae had died a few months earlier, news I had withheld because I wanted to tell it to her in person. She received it calmly, the way she had accepted Roy's death and my phone call telling her that we were both widows now.

Her most recent stroke had taken away her ability to speak clearly. She communicated with smiles, or arranged her face in a frown, but neither smiles nor frowns had much to do with what anyone said to her.

The nursing home staff was fond of her because Pat was the only patient who never complained.

She seemed pleased to see me, if not entirely sure who I was. A radio played somewhere inside, and she hummed tunelessly along with the music and moved her swollen, slippered feet, a seventy-two-year-old former dancer, who in some core of herself was still a dancer. "I guess I ought to tell you that Cy died too," I said. I thought Pat was entitled to know, and that this knowledge could not touch her because nothing could. As we sat together, her glance had flicked off me and the cars in the parking lot with equal disinterest.

She turned and stared at me, through glasses smeary with thumbprints, and made a sound I interpreted as "What?" "He died, Mother," I said again. "He'd been sick for a long time. It's sad, isn't it? I'm sorry too."

The noise that ripped out of her throat froze me. "No!" My mother's hands jerked up from the arms of her chair and struck at me, catching a finger in one of my hoop earrings, and the keening sound poured out of her as I took the earring off and reached over to comfort her. Her face contorted, she batted my hands away.

"What *on earth* did you say to her?" asked the nurse who came running out to us, alarmed. I let her lead Pat inside and went and sat in my car, too shaken to start it and drive away.

I thought I had guessed correctly at what Pat had forgotten. I'd been massively wrong about what she remembered.

"She couldn't adjust to that life back on the road, with you," Ila Mae had told me, talking about her sister's early life. "Maybe Cy wouldn't come home all night, and that left her in some little room alone with you. She called me and said 'I don't know where Cy is and I haven't known for two days. Can you come over?' I came and got you, and we didn't see anything of him for two or three days. He'd been gambling in a crap game."

The Cy my mother mourned was not the man who parked her in motel rooms and disappeared, not the man who had blackened her eyes more than once, nor the man Cy became, the senior statesman of rodeo. Like me, she mourned another Cy entirely, the husband who had picked her up and carried her, when they danced the night away, because out of vanity she insisted on wearing shoes a size and a half too small. Nothing—not time, not Roy, not other losses—had erased that memory for her, any more than time had erased it for me.

I put this book aside finally, wondering if anyone ever makes sense of fathers, or families, and whether their daughters perceive all fathers as part men, part myth. Whoever the man with the golden voice was when he took his high-heeled boots off, and his tall hat, and the diamond horseshoe stick-pin, and the pearl buttons marching up to his elbows, I missed him when he unhitched our trailer in Billings decades ago. I missed him as a child and as an adult, every time I saw him and then didn't see him. And I go right on missing him, even as he eludes me again.

I tell myself that I would be less Cy-like if I had the chance to grow up all over again, less stubborn and more forgiving; that I'd judge Roy and Dorothy less harshly; that I'd understand my mother fully and tend the spark that remained in her, underneath the ashes. I'd do a better job of loving this time, and so would they, and we'd be that domestic group in the *Saturday Evening Post* covers, strangers to both reality and regret.

Then I realize there are no rodeo announcers in those illustrations, no soubrettes, no auburn-haired nurses and no earnest Old Honest Faces—also no daughters with the temperament of bulldogs. I accept the lot of us, at last, as who and what we were: just one more group of people joined together as that mysterious and complicated thing, a family.

About the Author

Cyra McFadden has written for *The New York Times*, *The Nation*, *Smithsonian* magazine, and many other publications. She now writes a biweekly column for the San Francisco *Examiner*.